BLIND SPOTS IN THE BIBLE

Text copyright © Adrian Plass 2006
The author asserts the moral right
to be identified as the author of this work

Published by
The Bible Reading Fellowship
First Floor, Elsfield Hall
15–17 Elsfield Way, Oxford OX2 8FG
Website: www.brf.org.uk

ISBN-10: 1 84101 505 9
ISBN-13: 978 1 84101 505 7
First published 2006
10 9 8 7 6 5 4 3 2 1 0
All rights reserved

Acknowledgments
Unless otherwise stated, scripture quotations are taken from the Holy Bible, New International
Version, copyright © 1973, 1978, 1984, 1995 by International Bible Society, are used by
permission of Hodder & Stoughton, a division of Hodder Headline Ltd. All rights reserved.
'NIV' is a registered trademark of International Bible Society. UK trademark number 1448790.

Scripture quotations taken from The Holy Bible, Today's New International Version. Copyright
© 2004 by International Bible Society. Used by permission of Hodder & Stoughton, a division
of Hodder Headline Ltd. All rights reserved. 'TNIV' is a registered trademark of International
Bible Society.

Scripture quotations taken from The New Revised Standard Version of the Bible, Anglicized
Edition, copyright © 1989, 1995 by the Division of Christian Education of the National
Council of the Churches of Christ in the USA, are used by permission. All rights reserved.

A catalogue record for this book is available from the British Library

Printed in Singapore by Craft Print International Ltd

BLIND SPOTS IN THE BIBLE

Puzzles and paradoxes that we tend to avoid

ADRIAN PLASS

This book is dedicated to my brave friend Liz Pierce, who has never allowed chronic suffering to dilute her generosity

Blind spot: an area in which a person lacks understanding or impartiality

THE CONCISE OXFORD DICTIONARY

CONTENTS

INTRODUCTION

This book is filled with what I have called 'blind spots' from the Bible. This does not necessarily mean that the quoted sections are obscure. Some passages will be very familiar to those with a reasonable working knowledge of scripture. The thing they have in common, as far as I am concerned, is at least one intriguing or disturbing aspect that I have previously missed, or noted out of the corner of my eye, but never got round to investigating or facing honestly. The Bible is fascinatingly full of such elements, and I could easily fill another couple of books. My guess is that they tend to accumulate because of laziness, because of my own fear, because of a blinkering overfamiliarity, and because of poorly informed, shallow teaching from the past.

It can be an extremely interesting and constructive exercise to root out some of these half-perceived truths and examine them in the light of our full attention. The list will be different for each one of us, but I suspect that we are all likely to be amazed when we discover the extent to which we have been playing a game of theological Chinese whispers with our own understanding of many concepts, some of which occupy quite a central position in the Christian faith. Having said that, I certainly do not make that claim for all of the passages presented here. One or two, such as the mention of angels taking human wives in Genesis, were just too bizarre to miss, but even in that case I found myself driven, as ever, to the crucial conclusion that we can safely explore the strangest of avenues as long as we are safe in Jesus. That in itself is always a valuable lesson to relearn.

There are, of course, many biblical stories and ideas that we will never fully understand until the day when God himself provides the clarity that eludes us here. In the meantime, however, we are certainly allowed to think and analyse and question anything that strikes us as strange or inexplicable. Our love and respect for the word of God can only be enhanced by genuinely grappling with such challenges to our comprehension. Think how long the church had to wait for Martin Luther. Perhaps the time has come for some other temporarily puzzled Christian to help the church take another quantum leap in its perception of the truth. It could be you.

These shooting stars of scripture flew at me, in no particular order, from every corner of the biblical cosmos. For those who cannot live without organization, however, I have divided the book into sections, the contents of which do sometimes overlap. That's inevitable, I suppose, given the nature of God, the universe and everything. I do hope you enjoy and benefit from my 'blind spots', and I wish you a continuation of God's cheerful blessing as you investigate your own.

THE REAL NATURE
OF JESUS

SERVICE WASH?

So he got up from the meal, took off his outer clothing, and wrapped a towel around his waist. After that, he poured water into a basin and began to wash his disciples' feet, drying them with the towel that was wrapped around him.

He came to Simon Peter, who said to him, 'Lord, are you going to wash my feet?'

Jesus replied, 'You do not realize now what I am doing, but later you will understand.'

'No,' said Peter, 'you shall never wash my feet.'

Jesus answered, 'Unless I wash you, you have no part with me.'

'Then, Lord,' Simon Peter replied, 'not just my feet but my hands and my head as well!'

Jesus answered, 'Those who have had a bath need only to wash their feet; their whole body is clean. And you are clean, though not every one of you.' For he knew who was going to betray him, and that was why he said not every one was clean.

When he had finished washing their feet, he put on his clothes and returned to his place. 'Do you understand what I have done for you?' he asked them. 'You call me "Teacher" and "Lord", and rightly so, for that is what I am. Now that I, your Lord and Teacher, have washed your feet, you also should wash one another's feet. I have set you an example that you should do as I have done for you. Very truly I tell you, servants are not greater than their master, nor are messengers greater than the one who sent them. Now that you know these things, you will be blessed if you do them.'
JOHN 13:4–17 (TNIV)

This passage is about a phenomenon that more and more tennis players are relying on nowadays, namely, the power of service. In case you missed it, that was a joke.

The Church as a whole (myself included, and this is my blind spot) has always had a rather affectionate relationship with this famous story of Jesus washing the disciples' feet. It has perhaps been regarded in the same way that we might regard a role play. Jesus stepped aside from his normal leadership role in order to provide the disciples with a little picture or illustration of the value of service. No one is so elevated or important, he was saying, that they could expect to escape the duty of service to others.

This is a very pale and subtly diluted version of the truth.

Jesus had no need to role-play humility and a desire to serve others. The king of heaven became a man in order that he could serve and save those whom he loved to the point of death—those who were and are heading full tilt towards a tragedy that we cannot begin to understand, disaster on a scale that will cause even the worst earthly calamity to pale into insignificance. The servant king put his heart as well as his back into the task that confronted him, and he certainly could not have accomplished it if the very tissues of his body had not been suffused with a wholly genuine desire to tie the shoelaces of the world, and even be nailed to a cross if it would help.

Be warned: Jesus in us will not be acting out service to others. He will be living it, and there will be no question of making exceptions to that duty of service for reasons that would never be allowed houseroom in the kingdom of God. I have done it myself so many times.

'I have tried to go on forgiving him, but quite honestly it wears me out and I see no point in letting it affect everything else, so I'm just leaving it for a while…'

'I'm all for service to others, but I've never been very good at that sort of thing, so I think I'll give it a miss…'

'I feel as if everyone wants a part of me. I think it's about time I carved out some space for myself and let the others get on with it…'

The trouble with all comments of this kind is that they sound very reasonable, and invariably contain a kernel of truth. If, for instance, the necessity to forgive the same person repeatedly is wearing us out, then we do need to look clearly at what is happening and perhaps make some changes. But, as we learn from the teaching of Jesus, we are not going to be released from our obligation to extend forgiveness continually to those who are truly sorry for hurting or offending us, even if they do exactly the same thing the next day.

Similarly, it is always tempting to stay within our comfort zones, and on one level it does make sense to stick to doing the things we are good at. There is no intrinsic value in doing things badly. But the life of service that Jesus is talking about cannot be run on those lines. There will be times when we have to plunge in and do the thing that is required, however unfamiliar and threatening it may be. Perhaps we will need to ask for advice and guidance from people who have previously been in the habit of seeking help and advice from us. Not always easy, is it?

Of course everyone wants a part of us. If we are serious about following Jesus in the way that this passage suggests, then there will be lots of parts of us available to everyone. We have to be careful to allow time for healthy relaxation and the needs of those close to us, as Jesus always did, but yes, we will be parcelled out for the benefit of others. No one ever said it would be easy. No one ever said it wouldn't be hard work.

A minister I know told me about a man who, in this respect, went through the same cycle again and again. He would gradually increase his input into one or more useful activities initiated by his church, and then abruptly announce that he was withdrawing because 'my family are just as important as anyone else, and they are the ones who are beginning to lose out'. This sounds so reasonable and responsible and carefully considered, doesn't it? Well, perhaps it was the first time—possibly even the second. But as time went by, this chap's family began to look more and more like a 'foxhole', the sort of refuge you leap into to avoid the heat of battle.

These things are not easy, are they? We all fall short. We all kid ourselves at times, and we all go through stages of laziness and resentment. But we want to be good, don't we? We want to be followers of the servant king, and make him proud of us. We must look after each other, and pray for each other, and encourage each other, and give each other a kick up the backside if necessary, and keep a sense of humour and perspective about it all. God will help us to be more like his Son.

A question

Let's look at our hands. I mean it. Go on, you look at your hands, and I will abandon the keyboard for a moment and look at mine. Here is the question we need to ask. Is he allowed full use of them?

—————— ❖ ——————

DEAR JOHN...

When John heard in prison what Christ was doing, he sent his disciples to ask him, 'Are you the one who was to come, or should we expect someone else?'

Jesus replied, 'Go back and report to John what you hear and see. The blind receive sight, the lame walk, those who have leprosy are cured, the deaf hear, the dead are raised, and the good news is preached to the poor. Blessed is anyone who does not fall away on account of me.'

As John's disciples were leaving, Jesus began to speak to the crowd about John: 'What did you go out into the desert to see? A reed swayed by the wind? If not, what did you go out to see? A man dressed in fine clothes? No, those who wear fine clothes are in kings' palaces. Then what did you go out to see? A prophet? Yes, I tell you, and more than a prophet. This is the one about whom it is written: "I will send my messenger ahead of you, who will prepare your way before you."

'I tell you the truth: among those born of women there has not risen anyone greater than John the Baptist; yet whoever is least in the kingdom of heaven is greater than he. From the days of John the Baptist until now, the kingdom of heaven has been forcefully advancing, and forceful men lay hold of it. For all the Prophets and the Law prophesied until John. And if you are willing to accept it, he is the Elijah who was to come. Those who have ears, let them hear.'

MATTHEW 11:2–15

It is generally expected, quite reasonably of course, that as we read about Jesus our reverence and love for him will grow. I agree with that. Certain moments in the Gospels, however, have a slightly different effect. They cause us to *like* him. Here is such a moment, and it involves Jesus in deliberately making a statement that he knows to be untrue. Now, if that's not a blind spot, I don't know what is. All right, you can excommunicate me in a minute. Just let me explain the context first.

I love this whole passage about John the Baptist. I've written about it many times—too many times, probably. I love the spiritual and personal passion throbbing beneath the words that Jesus declares to the crowd about his imprisoned, troubled cousin. I think that Jesus loved John. Apart from anything else, John was, at this time, the only one of Jesus' contemporaries who came anywhere near being as specifically driven and fuelled by the desire to obey God as he was. The idea of this good servant lying in darkness, asking himself if he had got it all wrong after all, would have caused Jesus great distress, not least because, as he later made clear to Peter when he was arrested in the garden, he could call on legions of angels if he wished and the situation could be changed in an instant.

Why did he not use the power available to him to save John? He could have, but he didn't. Why not? I guess the answer is that, unlike most of us, Jesus was never motivated by sentimentalism or personal preference. He was engaged in the most important three-year period of work in the history of the world, and nothing could be allowed to impede the completion of that task. As we know, Peter

14

learned a severe lesson on this very subject after rebuking Jesus for announcing that he would die in the near future.

No, much as Jesus probably longed to rescue John, he could not see such an initiative within his Father's will, and therefore it was not going to happen. John was going to stay where he was. It was part of the plan.

Incidentally, it might be worth pointing out that we really are not very good at this sort of thing nowadays. There is an automatic assumption that difficulty or hardship must be avoided altogether, or escaped from at the earliest opportunity. Very understandable, of course, but not necessarily in tune with the will of God, who is still asking us to prioritize his plans rather than our own.

Here's a brief example. When Terry Waite, the Archbishop of Canterbury's special envoy, was taken hostage in the Middle East in 1987, there was a great deal of prayer for his swift release. Absolutely right: we should always ask God for a cup of suffering to be removed if possible, and sometimes, thank God, that wish is granted. The thing that I missed in this case was any acknowledgment that Terry Waite might be in precisely the right place at the right time and in contact with the right people.

We are quite happy to accept that the apostle Paul needed to be shipwrecked and beaten and starved in the course of his ministry to the Gentiles, and we know in our hearts that if he had not been willing (and allowed by God) to suffer these things, the Christian Church would have lacked the growth and enrichment that his extraordinary life and work brought to it. I feel sure that Paul himself would have valued prayers for his physical safety, but only if they were accompanied by equally fervent prayers that he should stay in the centre of the Lord's will, whatever the implications of that might be.

Clearly, there was to be no intervention, miraculous or otherwise, in the imprisonment of John. All Jesus could do was to send a carefully worded communication to his cousin, one that contained three very significant messages.

First, John should take note of the fact that healings were taking place in parallel with the preaching of the good news of salvation. These were signs that the Son of God had arrived on the earth. Since before his conception it had been known that John was destined to prepare the way for the Messiah. Until now, he had carried out his task well, and on that sparkling day in the distant past when Jesus had come to be baptized by his cousin in the River Jordan, John had been filled with confident, prophetic certainty. Now that certainty was gone, and it needed to be rekindled.

Second, Jesus says that those who do not stumble on his account are blessed by God. 'Look, John,' he seems to be saying, 'I know things are tough, but stick in there. Don't give up. A day is coming when you will be so glad that you remained obedient to the end. Be strong. God will bless you. I bless you.'

The third message brings us at last to this business of Jesus saying something that is not actually true. Have you ever wondered why the writer of this account recorded the fact that Jesus started to speak to the crowd as John's disciples were leaving? No? Neither had I. Could it be that Jesus wanted those disciples to overhear the wonderful things he was about to say about their master, and perhaps particularly these words: 'Among those born of women there has not risen anyone greater than John the Baptist.'

Just think about that statement for a moment. Is it true? No, of course it's not. And John would have known that perfectly well as the words were repeated to him by his disciples back in the dismal confines of Herod's prison. They might have brought a smile to his face for the first time in days. They almost certainly made him cry.

Very nice of Jesus.

A prayer

Father, we know that every one of us has a job to do for you. Sometimes it gets tough and we feel like opting out, or we lose confidence in our relationship with you and in those precious moments of certainty that we have known in the past. Thank you that Jesus says the same to us as he said to his cousin all those years ago. 'Look at what I have done in the past and what I am doing now. Stay strong and be blessed. You are a very special person.' Thank you for the humanity of Jesus, and for his generosity of spirit towards John and towards us.

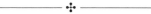

THE SADNESS OF IT ALL

When the Jews who had been with Mary in the house, comforting her, noticed how quickly she got up and went out, they followed her, supposing she was going to the tomb to mourn there.

When Mary reached the place where Jesus was and saw him, she fell at his feet and said, 'Lord, if you had been here, my brother would not have died.'

When Jesus saw her weeping, and the Jews who had come along with her also weeping, he was deeply moved in spirit and troubled. 'Where have you laid him?' he asked.

'Come and see, Lord,' they replied.

Jesus wept.

Then the Jews said, 'See how he loved him!'

But some of them said, 'Could not he who opened the eyes of the blind man have kept this man from dying?'

JOHN 11:31–37

Who am I to interpret the tears of Jesus? Nobody. But I shall try, of course. The Bible is there for us to use and question and to give us understanding.

Why was Jesus weeping?

Many have asked the question, and we have been offered a multitude of answers. Never mind; all can be useful or illuminating. Here is the light that shines on me today. There is an aching truth at the centre of this, the shortest verse in the Bible, that I have often seen out of the corner of my eye but never quite had the courage to face properly. And it really does require courage. Why? Well, I would say that my role as an authentic and effective follower of Jesus in this world depends on understanding this truth and unreservedly applying it to my life. A bit of an exaggeration? Sounds like it, doesn't it? If only that were so.

Jesus was weeping because he had been obliged to do what he was told. Jesus was weeping because the divine imperative had been crystal clear. There was to be no hurried trip to Bethany in order to be there in time to heal Lazarus before he died. Jesus was weeping because, although he had made the right decision, the necessary dislocation of earth and heaven was breaking his heart. Jesus was weeping because all the loves were tearing him apart and were about to spread him piecemeal across the universe.

Having started to understand this, do I still want to identify with him? I need to grasp the fact that if Jesus wept, then I shall too, if I truly wish to follow his example. There was a phase in our lives when Bridget and I subscribed fairly blindly to the proposition that Christian living was, broadly speaking, an optimistic sort of affair. After all, it was only a matter of time before Jesus would return and sort everything out and all we believers would be swept up into glory. In the meantime, we could sing triumphant hymns and choruses, rejoice in the knowledge that we were saved, do our best to save a few more, and be as kind and helpful to others as possible.

It was as though we had never read the Gospels, as though we had never really paid attention to all those stories and words of Jesus that are almost too familiar to be perceived clearly. Of course the Master had his overtly happy and even ecstatic moments, and there was certainly a dimension of quiet, immovable joy in his spirit. It was this joy that he so wanted to leave with his followers, as we discover in the 17th chapter of John's Gospel, when Jesus prays to his Father about the disciples. 'I am coming to you now, but I say these things while I am still in the world, so that they may have the full measure of my joy within them' (v. 13).

So, yes, of course he knew what it was to be happy and to be filled with joy, and in theory nobody ever had better reason to be optimistic and positive than Jesus, the Son of God, who knew where he had come from since before the world began, and had no doubt about where he would be going when his time on earth came to an end. And yet the most cursory reading of the Gospels reveals a man whose ministry was shot through with pain, frustration, disappointment and a fair measure of emotion—an aspect of human experience that we have so often been warned against.

Let's just remind ourselves of a few of these painful times in the life of Jesus, and the comments of other biblical writers on the same subject. Take your time. I found myself shedding a few tears as I typed out this selection of passages. Don't worry if you do the same. I suspect that it's quite good for us.

He was despised and rejected by men, a man of sorrows, and familiar with suffering. Like one from whom men hide their faces he was despised, and we esteemed him not.
ISAIAH 53:3

For we do not have a high priest who is unable to sympathize with our weaknesses, but we have one who has been tempted in every way, just as we are—yet was without sin.
HEBREWS 4:15

During the days of Jesus' life on earth, he offered up prayers and petitions with loud cries and tears to the one who could save him from death, and he was heard because of his reverent submission. Although he was a son, he learned obedience from what he suffered and, once made perfect, he became the source of eternal salvation for all who obey him.
HEBREWS 5:7–9

As he approached Jerusalem and saw the city, he wept over it.
LUKE 19:41

'O Jerusalem, Jerusalem, you who kill the prophets and stone those sent to you, how often I have longed to gather your children together, as a hen gathers her chicks under her wings, but you were not willing! Look, your house is left to you desolate. I tell you, you will not see me again until you say, "Blessed is he who comes in the name of the Lord."'
LUKE 13:34–35

From this time many of his disciples turned back and no longer followed him. 'You do not want to leave me too, do you?' Jesus asked the Twelve. Simon Peter answered him, 'Lord, to whom shall we go? You have the words of eternal life. We believe and know that you are the Holy One of God.'
JOHN 6:66–69

'Now my heart is troubled, and what shall I say? "Father, save me from this hour"? No, it was for this very reason I came to this hour. Father, glorify your name!'
JOHN 12:27–28

When they came to the disciples, they saw a great crowd around them, and some scribes arguing with them. When the whole crowd saw him, they were immediately overcome with awe, and they ran forward to greet him. He asked them, 'What are you arguing about with them?' Someone from the crowd answered him, 'Teacher, I brought you my son; he has a spirit that makes him unable to speak; and whenever it seizes him, it dashes him down; and he foams and grinds his teeth and becomes rigid; and I asked your disciples to cast it out, but they could not do so.' He answered them, 'You faithless generation, how much longer must I be among you? How much longer must I put up with you? Bring him to me.' And they brought the boy to him.
MARK 9:14–20a (NRSV)

They went to a place called Gethsemane; and he said to his disciples, 'Sit here while I pray.' He took with him Peter and James and John, and began to be distressed and agitated. And he said to them, 'I am deeply grieved,

even to death; remain here, and keep awake.' And going a little farther, he threw himself on the ground and prayed that, if it were possible, the hour might pass from him. He said, 'Abba, Father, for you all things are possible; remove this cup from me; yet, not what I want, but what you want.' He came and found them sleeping; and he said to Peter, 'Simon, are you asleep? Could you not keep awake one hour? Keep awake and pray that you may not come into the time of trial; the spirit indeed is willing, but the flesh is weak.' And again he went away and prayed, saying the same words. And once more he came and found them sleeping, for their eyes were very heavy; and they did not know what to say to him. He came a third time and said to them, 'Are you still sleeping and taking your rest? Enough! The hour has come; the Son of Man is betrayed into the hands of sinners. Get up, let us be going. See, my betrayer is at hand.'
MARK 14:32–42 (NRSV)

'My God, my God, why have you forsaken me?'
MATTHEW 27:46b

Do I still want to follow Jesus after reading all that? Well, I think I do, but I am going to have to allow a truth that I thought I had already absorbed to sink more deeply into my understanding. Put at its simplest, it is this. If we do not do what we see the Father doing, we are wasting our time, but, whatever anyone says, there will be days when the sadness of it all will make us weep.

A prayer
Give us the courage, Lord, to be obedient even when it hurts us and seems unloving to others. Help us to keep our eyes on you and our feet on the road that you choose for us. The distractions are powerful, and some of them seem so right. May we learn to hold in tension the confidence we have in you and the pain involved in following Jesus. Hold us, Lord, in your will.

TRICKS AND STONES
MAY BREAK MY BONES...

At dawn he appeared again in the temple courts, where all the people gathered round him, and he sat down to teach them. The teachers of the law and the Pharisees brought in a woman caught in adultery. They made her stand before the group and said to Jesus, 'Teacher, this woman was caught in the act of adultery. In the Law Moses commanded us to stone such women. Now what do you say?' They were using this question as a trap, in order to have a basis for accusing him.

But Jesus bent down and started to write on the ground with his finger. When they kept on questioning him, he straightened up and said to them, 'If any one of you is without sin, let him be the first to throw a stone at her.' Again he stooped down and wrote on the ground.

At this, those who heard began to go away one at a time, the older ones first, until only Jesus was left, with the woman still standing there. Jesus straightened up and asked her, 'Woman, where are they? Has no one condemned you?'

'No one, sir,' she said.

'Then neither do I condemn you,' Jesus declared. 'Go now and leave your life of sin.'

JOHN 8:2–11

Does the Bible ever fill you with joy? I suppose the PC (Pharisaically Correct) reply to that is, 'Oh, yes, it certainly does! All of it, all the time.' Absolute rubbish, of course, but since when have we let a little thing like dishonesty come between fellowshipping Christians?

The Bible does fill me with joy sometimes. Not frequently, but often enough to keep me curious and concentrated. There are two blind spots in this passage, and the first of them is really lifting my spirits as I think through and around it.

It had never occurred to me, you see, to ask myself why the teachers of the law and the Pharisees were so sure that their question about the woman who had committed adultery would be a useful trap for snaring Jesus and giving them a reason (or an excuse) for publicly accusing him. Certainly he had challenged the popular understanding of Mosaic Law on one or two points.

Divorce is one example. You can read about it in the 19th chapter of Matthew's Gospel. In yet another attempt to test Jesus publicly, the Pharisees ask if it is lawful for a man to divorce his wife for 'any and every reason'. Hearing the reply that Jesus gives about the permanence of marriage, they play what they clearly think is their winning card. 'Why then... did Moses command that a man give his wife a certificate of divorce and send her away?' (Matthew 19:7). Jesus then refers them to a much older and more fundamental truth that is based on love rather than law. It was, he explains, because the hearts of men had become hard that Moses permitted them to divorce in his lifetime. No doubt the Pharisees found this answer annoying in the extreme, and it must have further fuelled their determination to catch him out at some later date.

Despite these instances of clarification and redefinition, however, it would be quite wrong to suppose that Jesus was setting out to attack or destroy the law. Some contemporary would-be religious anarchists, such as the Zealots, probably hoped that he was. On the contrary, earlier in Matthew's Gospel, Jesus makes what may have been a very impassioned speech on the subject.

Do not think that I have come to abolish the Law or the Prophets; I have not come to abolish them but to fulfil them. I tell you the truth, until heaven and earth disappear, not the smallest letter, not the least stroke of a pen, will by any means disappear from the Law until everything is accomplished. Anyone who breaks one of the least of these commands and teaches others to do the same will be called least in the kingdom of heaven, but whoever practises and teaches these commands will be called great in the kingdom of heaven. For I tell you that unless your

righteousness surpasses that of the Pharisees and the teachers of the law, you
will certainly not enter the kingdom of heaven.
MATTHEW 5:17–20

So there we have it. Jesus was definitely opposed to sterile manipulation of a law that was born out of love, but he is an upholder of that law, and Moses certainly ruled that a woman taken in adultery should be stoned. So what made the Pharisees and the teachers of the law so certain that Jesus would oppose the carrying out of this particular, perfectly legal penalty? It is the answer to this question that makes my heart sing.

The same musical thing happens to my heart when I read about the widow of Nain, and about Peter running to the shore when he sees that the Lord he loves is waiting for him, and about the servant in the garden who lost and gained an ear within a matter of seconds, and about the men who were prayed for when they nailed Jesus to the cross, and about that last-minute arrangement, in the midst of unspeakable pain, for Mary to go and live with John, one of the disciples with whom Jesus had the closest relationship.

The answer to the question, if you can remember what it was after all this, is that those Pharisees had learned, whether they liked it or not, purely by day-to-day observation, what kind of man Jesus was. Simple as that, really. They knew in their hearts and they hated it— and I know in my heart and I love it, and I hope you know in your heart and rejoice in it—that this man, who happened to be God, could never in a million years have sat back and watched a woman being stoned to death if there was anything at all he could do to prevent it happening, law or no law. And it is interesting, is it not, that Jesus never actually argued the point with his questioners. What he did do was to find a way to save her, not just from a dreadful fate at the hands of her executioners but also from her sin. Neat. Perfect.

That brings us to the second of my blind spots. Jesus suggested that anyone who had never sinned should throw the first stone. And, of course, there was nobody there who fitted into that category— nobody, that is, except Jesus himself. He was without sin. He could have thrown the first stone. Why did he not? In a way, we have already answered that question, but the implications of the complete answer are immense. I shall leave you to think that through for yourself, but in the meantime let us use a little imagination. How might the woman in the story have told the tale of her escape from stoning in later years? A little like this, perhaps.

It didn't matter how long those Pharisees and teachers and people poked their irritable questions at the silent man writing in the dust with his finger. None of that mattered. I knew I was going to die. I was already trembling with fear, trying not to imagine those first sharp lumps of stone smashing into my arms and legs as I tried to cover my face. I knew I wouldn't be strong enough to protect my head for long. The bones would break, and after that I would just pray to be knocked unconscious, and hope to die really quickly without ever waking up to more pain.

Thinking of my parents' grief and shame was the worst thing. It made me want to weep and scream, but I was locked up tight inside myself. Couldn't make a sound. I almost wished the talking would stop and they'd just get on with it.

Then came a moment when the strange man said something that I couldn't quite hear, and a silence fell. That was when I screwed my eyes tight shut and waited for it to start. But nothing happened. When I dared to look again, everything seemed to be frozen, like a picture. No one spoke or moved for several seconds, then one of the greybeards turned his back and a rock dropped from his hand and thumped on to the ground. He just walked quietly away towards the town without looking back. Then another, and another, and yet another, stone after stone landing with little splashes of dust as they went, until only the youngest, noisiest questioners remained. I saw fury and disappointment on their faces, but even they scratched their heads and stomped off at last, one or two of them throwing their arms angrily in the air as they went.

There was only that man and me left in the end. So strange. He looked around with a frown for a second, as if he was surprised to see no one there, then he gazed straight into my eyes and said, 'It's gone very quiet. Does not one of that baying pack condemn you?'

I gulped like a fish caught in a net. Still had trouble finding my voice. 'No, sir,' I managed to whisper at last. 'I don't think so. They've all gone.'

He did a very peculiar thing then. He lifted one hand and he flicked a tiny little pebble in my direction so that it landed just in front of my feet.

'Well, in that case,' he said, smiling really nicely at me, 'I don't either. You'd better get home. And you will sort your life out, won't you?'

When he said that, he made me feel as if I could. And, as a matter of record, I did.

A prayer

Thank you for being that sort of person, Lord Jesus. Thank you for revealing the nature of God to us, for allowing us to see, just as the Pharisees and teachers saw with such chagrin all those years ago, that you are a God of kindness and compassion, caring about all those who suffer. Assist us in reflecting that loving attitude to others.

Thank you also, Lord, for not condemning us because we are sinners. We are truly sorry that we consistently fail to reach your mark. Teach us to know, as the woman in this story must have known, that change is actually possible, especially when we have learned that we really are forgiven and loved.

BODY LANGUAGE

From there he set out and went away to the region of Tyre. He entered a house and did not want anyone to know he was there. Yet he could not escape notice, but a woman whose little daughter had an unclean spirit immediately heard about him, and she came and bowed down at his feet. Now the woman was a Gentile, of Syrophoenician origin. She begged him to cast the demon out of her daughter. He said to her, 'Let the children be fed first, for it is not fair to take the children's food and throw it to the dogs.' But she answered him, 'Sir, even the dogs under the table eat the children's crumbs.' Then he said to her, 'For saying that, you may go—the demon has left your daughter.' So she went home, found the child lying on the bed, and the demon gone.

MARK 7:24–30 (NRSV)

This is one of those passages that continually suggest new ideas or angles of thought and approach. I have written all sorts of things about these verses over the years, but I have never consciously focused on the dominant response that it evokes in me. This is true for so much of my contact with the Bible. The same may be true for you. There has always been a temptation to edit out my first, spontaneous reaction to certain passages, especially when that reaction seems to be critical or disrespectful of one or more members of the Trinity. I strongly resist that temptation nowadays because I am beginning to understand that Jesus was absolutely right when he said that honesty will liberate us (John 8:32).

Why is Jesus so *horribly* rude to this poor, desperate woman who had come to find help and healing for her beloved daughter? What is the matter with him? Fancy suggesting that giving her what she wants is like throwing food to the dogs. Come on! There is no excuse, is there? Not for the Son of God. What do you think?

Well, I suppose on the face of it there could be a sort of justification. As we can see from the opening verses of the passage, Jesus seems to have been looking forward to a day off from the constant stream of people asking for help and healing. No one was supposed to know where he was, and suddenly, in the middle of one of his all-too-rare respite periods, this tiresome Gentile woman appears, having successfully tracked him down in the hope that he might do something for her daughter. Well, everyone needs a day off now and then, don't they? Jesus can have been no exception. Maybe he forgot himself for a moment and expressed his frustration more irritably than would normally have been the case—perfectly understandable.

No. No, it's not. This is Jesus, and he was without sin. I truly believe that. I have quite frequently been guilty of petulant outbursts in tiring or stressful situations, but I am just a common-or-garden follower of Jesus. I sin continually and have to be forgiven continually. Jesus was not like that. I expect he was very tired, and he may well have sighed wearily on discovering that it was to be business as usual, but I cannot believe that he would have allowed that weariness to spill over as bad temper. No, that won't work. It didn't happen.

What about the cultural context and problems with translation and all that? Well, perhaps experts would like to explain to me that unkindness was regarded as a virtue in that age, and that the original Greek words carry a very strong sense of wanting to buy the woman an ice cream and lay on free transport back to Syrophoenicia—but I wouldn't listen to them if they did. No, there has to be something else.

So what might that something be? My wife supplied a possible clue just the other day. She happened to be talking about this passage, and the term she used in connection with it was 'body language'. Interesting. I have a friend who suffered spinal injuries in a car accident years ago. As a result, she is confined to a wheelchair. She has also lost the use of many of her facial muscles. She can speak, albeit in a virtual monotone, but she is unable to show any trace of expression on her face. Here is a humorous, witty person who loves to chat and banter, but she will never actually smile or frown or giggle again. All those things going on inside, and a complete lack of body language with which to express them. People misjudge her constantly.

The Gospels are a little bit like that. Literary conventions of the time are such that we are allowed very little information about the way in which speeches were actually delivered. There is almost nothing about expressions, gestures, pauses or particular vocal emphases. Let us have a go at retelling this story from Mark's Gospel using a little semi-educated guesswork.

Jesus enters the house of a generous supporter in Tyre, hoping that his arrival in the town has not been noticed. He is racked with tiredness after ministering to the crowds of people who have constantly petitioned him for healing. He has always been vividly conscious of power going out of him for the healing of even one person. Focusing on and dealing with the needs of hundreds has left him drained and seriously in need of a place to rest and gather strength. This house on this day might offer him exactly what he needs.

It is not to be. Moments after leaning back against the chair and allowing his eyes to close at last, he registers the fact that someone has entered the room. Raising his eyelids a millimetre or two, he finds that a woman is kneeling before him. Her clothes and manner betray her origins. She is not of the Jewish people. Looking into her face, he perceives intelligence, awareness and a burning passion that is obviously about to be expressed in words. For one moment his heart sinks, but what is temptation for, if not to be resisted? The moment quickly passes. Encounters such as this one are part of the reason for his coming, and, in any case, there is a quality in the woman that appeals to him on more than one level. He smiles a little at his own thoughts, leaning forward so that his elbows rest on his knees, his fingers steepled beneath his chin.

'What can I do for you?'

The story flies out of her like a storm. The unclean spirit. The demented girl. The horror. The heartbreak. The sudden hope. The decision to make a plea for help. He listens, nodding very slightly as she speaks. There is more than a hint of mutual understanding in the meeting of their eyes. Unconditional love, passion, determination, wit. These things they have in common.

'And perhaps, as a Gentile, you would care to explain to me,' he says in response, still with a smile on his lips, one eyebrow raised quizzically, 'why you suppose that I might be willing to take the children's food and throw it to the dogs?'

She does not disappoint him. A smile lights her face for the first time.

'Because, sir,' she says calmly, her eyes holding his, 'even the dogs eat the scraps that the children happen to drop under the table. Is that not so?'

He chuckles quietly. 'Yes, indeed they do. Very well said. Go home and look after your daughter. She's fine.'

After the woman has left, weeping with happiness, he leans back, closes his tired eyes once more and prays for strength. It is extremely unlikely that this woman's emotional exit from the house will go unnoticed. Very soon there will be others.

Pure conjecture, of course. I cannot possibly claim to know that the incident happened in this way. It is equally certain, however, that no one can possibly claim to know that it did not.

A prayer

Father, thank you for our freedom to ask questions and speculate. Help us to be brave and honest in our dealings with scripture, facing the things that trouble us and looking beyond the mere words to a truth that will offer us even greater freedom. Thank you for the challenge of this and all other stories that teach us more about Jesus. Thank you for the passion and determination with which he obeyed your will on this earth, pushing on beyond barriers of physical exhaustion and pain for our sake. We will try to understand just how intensive and complex that process was at times.

---------- ⁂ ----------

EVERYTHING SHE'D EVER DONE?

Now he had to go through Samaria. So he came to a town in Samaria called Sychar, near the plot of ground Jacob had given to his son Joseph. Jacob's well was there, and Jesus, tired as he was from the journey, sat down by the well. It was about noon.

When a Samaritan woman came to draw water, he said to her, 'Will you give me a drink?' (His disciples had gone into the town to buy food.)

The Samaritan woman said to him, 'You are a Jew and I am a Samaritan woman. How can you ask me for a drink?' (For Jews do not associate with Samaritans.)

Jesus answered her, 'If you knew the gift of God and who it is that asks you for a drink, you would have asked him and he would have given you living water.'

'Sir,' the woman said, 'you have nothing to draw with and the well is deep. Where can you get this living water? Are you greater than our father Jacob, who gave us the well and drank from it himself, as did also his sons and his flocks and herds?'

Jesus answered, 'Everyone who drinks this water will be thirsty again, but those who drink the water I give them will never thirst. Indeed the water I give them will become in them a spring of water welling up to eternal life.'

The woman said to him, 'Sir, give me this water so that I won't get thirsty and have to keep coming here to draw water.'

He told her, 'Go, call your husband and come back.'

'I have no husband,' she replied.

Jesus said to her, 'You are right when you say you have no husband. The fact is, you have had five husbands, and the man you now have is not your husband. What you have just said is quite true.'

'Sir,' the woman said, 'I can see that you are a prophet. Our ancestors worshipped on this mountain, but you Jews claim that the place where we must worship is in Jerusalem.'

'Woman,' Jesus replied, 'believe me, a time is coming when you will worship the Father neither on this mountain nor in Jerusalem. You Samaritans worship what you do not know; we worship what we do know, for salvation is from the Jews. Yet a time is coming and has now come when the true worshippers will worship the Father in the Spirit and in truth, for they are the kind of worshippers the Father seeks. God is spirit, and his worshippers must worship in spirit and in truth.'

The woman said, 'I know that Messiah' (called Christ) 'is coming. When he comes, he will explain everything to us.'

Then Jesus declared, 'I, the one speaking to you—I am he.'

Just then his disciples returned and were surprised to find him talking with a woman. But no one asked, 'What do you want?' or 'Why are you talking with her?'

Then, leaving her water jar, the woman went back to the town and said to the people, 'Come, see a man who told me everything I've ever done. Could this be the Messiah?' They came out of the town and made their way toward him.

JOHN 4:4–30 (TNIV)

What is it with Jesus and Samaritan women? On this occasion, just as with the Syrophoenician woman, he enters the picture in a state of extreme weariness. He then engages a non-Jewish female in a brief but highly significant conversation that is pretty well guaranteed to bring hordes of others rushing along to see and drain him for themselves. People often point out that Jesus made time to pray and to recuperate, and there is no doubt that he did do a lot of that, but I get the feeling he was never completely off duty.

I have included the whole text of this story for two reasons. First, apart from anything else, it is a fascinating scene for us to be allowed to witness. Do try to relax and read it properly from beginning to end. Enjoy every word of the dialogue. Take time, if you have it, to picture the flickering light and shadow of change on this woman's face as she shifts in her heart and mind from alarm to puzzlement to amazement to shame to sudden insight, and finally to the unrestrained excitement that causes her to abandon her water jar and rush back home to Sychar to spread the news. Be aware of and recreate the unwritten pauses, the gestures, the making and breaking of eye contact that must have occurred as the conversation developed and the Samaritan woman began to realize that this unexpected encounter with a man at a well was unlike any other she had known in the past.

The second reason for including so much of the story is connected with the blind spot that I have detected in myself when it comes to this particular passage. As you read through the account, you will note that Jesus displayed a knowledge about the woman at the well that he could not have acquired other than by spiritual insight. What exactly was this knowledge? He knew that she was not married because she told him so, but he also knew that she had actually been married five times, and that the man she lived with—her partner, I suppose we would call him now—was not her husband. He may have known other things about her, but they are not recorded here. He may have said additional things to her about her life, but again, if he did, we are not allowed to know what they were. What we do know is that when this woman arrived back in Sychar she announced that she had met a man who told her *everything she'd ever done*.

But he didn't, did he? Unless there really is lots of other stuff that we don't get to hear about, all he told her was that she had been married five times and was now living in a sinful situation with yet another man. That in itself was a major issue, of course, but it could hardly be regarded as sufficient evidence for claiming that he had told her *everything* she'd ever done.

That was my blind spot. Why did she make that claim? Perhaps it was merely the kind of exaggeration that anyone might be guilty of, on getting into a state of high excitement. Does it really matter?

I think it matters. Let's go back to the dialogue for a moment. The Samaritan woman has just begun, in a misty sort of way, to understand that this strange man is offering her something out of the ordinary. Failing to comprehend his reference to a spring of water welling up to eternal life, she appears to be expecting some kind of conjuring trick involving an endless supply of actual water. Presumably Jesus had such an air of authority that she felt this might be genuinely feasible.

Jesus meets her request with an apparent irrelevancy. 'Go and fetch your husband,' he suggests, 'and bring him back here.'

Did she stare at him for a moment or two at this juncture, weighing the rival merits of coming out with the whole dismal story or telling just enough of the truth to obscure the facts about her life? In the end she opts for the latter, and it is at this point that Jesus drops his bombshell. No, she certainly does not have a husband. Too right. She has had five husbands, and the man she is with now is not her husband at all.

This woman's reply to such devastatingly accurate insight sits on the page like a dull slab of prose, but in reality there can have been nothing dull about her response. Shock and horror at first, but then a breathless excitement gathers in her as she discovers that this man, this very man sitting here in front of her, is the Messiah, the expected one, the one from God who will explain everything. Not only does he know the very worst about her, but he has also indicated that if she wishes, she can ask him for the sort of water that will bring eternal life. She flies away homeward, overflowing with good news instead of water.

Jesus did not tell the woman at the well everything she had ever done, but he did do the same with her as he did with the rich young ruler, the cripple at the pool near the Sheep Gate, and the paralysed man who was let down through the roof by his friends. In all these cases, he spoke straight into a negative feature that was exercising a dominant role in their lives and needed to be removed before real progress could be made. For the rich young ruler it was an identity defined by wealth, for the cripple it was a question of whether or not he really did want to be healed, for the paralysed man it was unspecified sin in his life, and for the Samaritan woman it was this history of tangled relationships. The fact that Jesus knew and named the nagging nightmare in this woman's heart would have carried a strong implication that, in fact, he knew everything about her.

He told me everything I've ever done—well, he didn't, but he could have done if he'd wanted to…

A prayer

Lord Jesus, you still meet and talk with us, and your insight into our lives remains as keen and as accurate as ever. Lord, although we are Christians, some of us are still dominated by those nagging nightmares that prevent us from really getting anywhere. There will be those among us who have been engaged in dark and terrible things in secret, perhaps for a long time. Some may be married Christians who have become involved in adulterous relationships. Some of us have been tempted by dishonest ways of making money and can see no way of extricating ourselves from the tangle. Others have somehow lost sight of our faith and are now role-playing the whole thing while among other Christians.

There are so many different nightmares, so much trouble and strife, Lord, in the lives of us and our brothers and sisters. We pray for all who are wrestling with such things. We remind ourselves that you know exactly what is going on, and that, if you wished, you really could tell us everything we've ever done. You are waiting to refresh us with forgiveness and a new experience of the water of life. Give us the courage to come clean, to start again and to serve you in newness of life, just as we hope that the Samaritan woman did after her encounter with you. Thank you, Lord Jesus, for opening your arms to us second-, third- or fourth-time prodigals.

FOLLOWING FAITHFULLY

---- ⁍ ----

JUST ONE THING

As Jesus and his disciples were on their way, he came to a village where a woman named Martha opened her home to him. She had a sister called Mary, who sat at the Lord's feet listening to what he said. But Martha was distracted by all the preparations that had to be made. She came to him and asked, 'Lord, don't you care that my sister has left me to do the work by myself? Tell her to help me!'

'Martha, Martha,' the Lord answered, 'you are worried and upset about many things, but only one thing is needed. Mary has chosen what is better, and it will not be taken away from her.'

LUKE 10:38–42

Fascinating, isn't it? After myriad forests have been destroyed in the making of billions of commentaries, tracts, spiritual biographies, helpful 'how-to' books and Christian newspapers and magazines, we learn that the answer is really very simple. Centuries of sermons seem to fade into silence as we hear the voice of Jesus making this extraordinary statement that only one thing is needed. Now there's a blind spot if ever there was one. Why are we not all doing it, this one thing?

Not to worry. Now we know, so we can move forward. Right! Good! Let's get on with it, then. Let's identify clearly what the one thing is, and then we should be able to sort ourselves and the church out in next to no time. So what is the one thing? Well, read the passage. See for yourself. It's not very complicated. The one thing that is needed is to be close to Jesus. Mary wanted to be with him. She loved him. Sorted! Away we go. No more problems for any of us.

Why doesn't it work as easily as that? Why don't you and I do the one thing that will make all the difference to our own lives and the lives of our church communities? (You may have noticed that one of the few things Jesus and I have in common, apart from supporting the same football team, is our tendency to answer questions with questions.)

Do you actually love Jesus? Do you really, really want to be with him? Mary wasn't applying some kind of spiritual technique, you know. She adored him. In the past she had met him and talked to him and eaten with him, and all she wanted was to be with him. It was genuine. That's the trouble. It has to be genuine.

What can we do to achieve this? Well, here are one or two things that have helped me in the past. They are not meant to be a menu for success, and these suggestions may not all suit you, but that doesn't matter.

First, I have found aimless travel very helpful. Don't laugh! I'm serious. Long walks in quiet places, trips by bus or on the train or by car. We do far too much planning in our lives as it is. There can be real value in creating open-ended activities and politely asking Jesus to join us as we walk or drive or sit on public transport. Go nowhere and take him with you.

Second, join Jesus in his sufferings. Sympathize and weep with him. In an earlier part of this book, you will find a chapter triggered by the shortest verse in the Bible: 'Jesus wept'. Included in that chapter is a list of some of the Bible verses that allow us to be involved in the suffering heart of the Master while he walked the earth. Add to the list if you wish. Read through those references slowly and thoughtfully. Use them to deepen your understanding of the heart of this man of sorrows.

Third, make a conscious effort to ask for his perspective to inform and inspire you in all situations, including and especially the mundane ones. Visits to the supermarket, chores in the house, fishing trips, gardening, clubbing, evenings in the pub, meals out, hair appointments, anything and everything that you might do or get involved in. You never know what might happen.

Fourth, an obvious one—read the Gospels. Hear his voice. Be there as those miracles happen and those stories are told. Enjoy it. Get wrapped up in it. Sit at his feet—like Mary.

A thought and a prayer

God help us if we try to substitute religion for relationship. Techniques and systems have no spiritual value unless they begin in the heart. We really do want to become more like Mary. We want to be drawn, like her, to the only place in the world that is truly safe.

So many distractions, Lord. Such a temptation to lose ourselves in hard work or religion or any number of other things that may seem very worthwhile, but in the final analysis are worthless unless our absolute priority is to be with you. Help us to find the hushed place, the corner of this busy world where we can meet you and quietly bask in being with you. Thank you for being so ready to meet with us, Lord. We look forward to spending time with you.

⁘

THEY LAUGHED AT HIM

Then a man named Jairus, a synagogue leader, came and fell at Jesus' feet, pleading with him to come to his house because his only daughter, a girl of about twelve, was dying. As Jesus was on his way, the crowds almost crushed him...

Someone came from the house of Jairus, the synagogue leader. 'Your daughter is dead,' he said. 'Don't bother the teacher any more.'

Hearing this, Jesus said to Jairus, 'Don't be afraid; just believe, and she will be healed.'

When he arrived at the house of Jairus, he did not let anyone go in with him except Peter, John and James, and the child's father and mother. Meanwhile, all the people were wailing and mourning for her. 'Stop wailing,' Jesus said. 'She is not dead but asleep.'

They laughed at him, knowing that she was dead. But he took her by the hand and said, 'My child, get up!' Her spirit returned, and at once she stood up. Then Jesus told them to give her something to eat. Her parents were astonished, but he ordered them not to tell anyone what had happened.

LUKE 8:41–42, 49–56 (TNIV)

They laughed at him.

When you isolate those four words and gaze steadily at them, what are the ideas and feelings that fill your mind? I find myself wondering how these people were able to switch from wailing to laughter so very quickly. Was it that they were not truly sincere? Were they professional mourners, interrupted by this lunatic in the midst of a normal day's work? No wonder Jesus insisted that only the child's parents should enter the girl's room with him. At least their feelings would be genuine.

They laughed at him.

God had come to live among human beings and be one of them, and one day, when he came to rekindle the light of someone's life, they laughed at him. They laughed because he had said something extraordinarily silly. Fancy saying the girl was asleep when it was perfectly obvious that she was dead. Idiot! There he goes into the room with the parents and the two disciples. Here he comes out again, with a little girl who has woken up and needs feeding, and a mother and father filled with joy unspeakable.

They laughed at him.

They still laugh at him and his absurd claims about heaven and hell and eternity. Idiot! How do we feel as we stand beside him like those two disciples? Are we sheepish, slightly embarrassed?

I am sometimes. I don't want to be. I want to be bold and loyal and trusting. I want to see miracles. But I don't like being laughed at. Sometimes I have been appalled by my unwillingness to stand up and be counted when it comes to being identified with Christian things, but there are also times when I am simply confused. Let me give you an example.

In a town where Bridget and I used to live, there was a man who regularly stood on a wooden box in the shopping precinct so that he could preach loudly to passers-by about the need for them to repent and ask Jesus into their lives. Everything about this fellow was on the wild side. Hair, eyes, clothes—all kind of wild. His message was blunt, uncompromising, black and white, totally without frills. As people passed him, they would smile a little and shake their heads, presumably dismissing him as a loony. Children giggled behind their hands. Nobody ever seemed actually to stop and listen. They just laughed at him.

Frankly, I was embarrassed by the very thought that anyone might connect me with that man. But I felt guilty as well. For goodness' sake, the fellow was preaching stuff that I believed and wrote about. And he was doing it openly without fear—or, at least, without allowing fear to hold him back. I found it excruciating. The sound of this gentleman's stentorian voice in the distance as I neared the precinct never failed to throw me into a spin. Sometimes I would make a ludicrously wide detour in order to avoid passing in front of the wild preacher. What a wretched creeping thing I was!

So was I right? Or was I wrong? I used to dampen the fires of guilt by telling myself that my task was to present the sane, human face of Christianity, and that allowing myself to be associated with the man on the box would prejudice my own message about Jesus. Well, that may have been part of what was going on in my head, but I know exactly what was in my heart. It was a chicken. A great big, fat, clucking chicken.

They laughed at him.

I really do not want to be one of 'them', and I am still not convinced that standing on a box to preach in the marketplace is necessarily the right way to go, but I am aware of a defensively motivated desire to represent Jesus on my own terms, and it troubles me.

A prayer

Lord Jesus, lead us through the mockery into the miracle. I am sometimes ashamed of my own lack of courage and loyalty. Forgive me for those times when I have been weak and spineless. I don't want to do silly, useless things just for the sake of it, but I do pray for strength to stand proudly for you when I am challenged, in any situation that you have chosen, however embarrassing or inappropriate it may seem at the time.

———————— ✢ ————————

COUCH POTATOES NEED NOT APPLY

'Anyone who receives you receives me, and anyone who receives me receives the one who sent me. Anyone who receives a prophet as a prophet will receive a prophet's reward, and anyone who receives a righteous person as a righteous person will receive a righteous person's reward. And if anyone gives even a cup of cold water to one of these little ones who is my disciple, I tell you the truth, that person will certainly be rewarded.'
MATTHEW 10:40–42

I have previously failed to notice something very helpful in this short section of Matthew's Gospel, but a warning is needed as well. Here is the helpful bit.

Many people suffer from feelings of spiritual inferiority. They are undoubtedly followers of Jesus, but practical circumstances such as ill health or heavy and unavoidable family commitments mean that they cannot get out and be part of what appear to be the more active and upfront aspects of Christian service. We pay lip service to the idea that there is no distinction between practical responsibilities and overtly religious activity, but accepting this as a fact is not always easy. Thrill-a-minute testimony books don't help. When your major efforts are going into getting your aged mother on to a commode, or shopping for six, or dealing with your own chronic ill health, accounts of someone else's miracle-strewn walk with God can be depressing, to say the least.

My friend Phyllis is a very good example. Phyllis, a faithful member of our church, celebrated her 89th birthday just a few days ago as I write, and has all sorts of ailments, including heart trouble and a badly degenerated hip that will have to be replaced before long. Originally a member of the Bible study group that we belong to, she rarely goes out in the evening nowadays and is unable to be involved in most of the physical activities that were once part of her life. She loves and is greatly loved by her family, but I think the limitations of age and illness are burdensome to her.

I wish that Phyllis understood the importance of the role she plays in our lives and the lives of many others in our church. She is a prayer warrior of the old school. She intercedes daily, not just for Bridget and me in all the work that we undertake, but also for our four children, all of whom have left home now. The knowledge that folk like Phyllis are continually holding us up before God gives a real buoyancy to the little boat in which we face the storms of life. She is as much a part of the crew as if she were physically travelling with us on the journey. We thank God for her, and for all those like her who take on the crucial task of support through prayer.

Well, just for people like Phyllis, and for all those who faithfully do what they can when they can, here is a little bit of good news. Jesus tells us in this passage that if we support another Christian who is engaged in any kind of Christian ministry, it is as though we ourselves are engaged in that same activity. Let us remind ourselves that Jesus always meant what he said. These are not word games. I repeat: anyone who upholds another person with prayer or finance or hospitality in his or her work for God will be regarded and rewarded as though they are doing the work of that person themselves. So help yourself to any job you want. You are greatly needed, and you will be very highly valued by God himself and by those whom you bless with your service.

The warning is simple. This offer is not extended to the mean-spirited, or to chronic couch potatoes. Please do not apply.

A prayer

Lord, we want to serve. Thank you that, no matter what our circumstances, we can all have an equal role. Help us to believe and understand that in our service to others we really are putting ourselves in the front line of the spiritual battle. Forgive us, Father, for doubting that you have a purpose for all of us. We pray for those who have begun to believe that their lives as useful Christians are over. Show them where their particular support is needed, whether it is in terms of prayer or money or encouragement. And we especially thank you, Father, for those prayer heroes like Phyllis who have steadfastly upheld your people through storms and sunshine, without ever expecting reward or recognition. We know that you will personally thank them one day.

---- ❖ ----

WHY NOT ALL OF US?

'I too was convinced that I ought to do all that was possible to oppose the name of Jesus of Nazareth. And that is just what I did in Jerusalem. On the authority of the chief priests I put many of the Lord's people in prison, and when they were put to death, I cast my vote against them. Many a time I went from one synagogue to another to have them punished, and I tried to force them to blaspheme. I was so obsessed with persecuting them that I even hunted them down in foreign cities.

'On one of these journeys I was going to Damascus with the authority and commission of the chief priests. About noon, King Agrippa, as I was on the road, I saw a light from heaven, brighter than the sun, blazing around me and my companions. We all fell to the ground, and I heard a voice saying to me in Aramaic, "Saul, Saul, why do you persecute me? It is hard for you to kick against the goads."

'Then I asked, "Who are you, Lord?"

'"I am Jesus, whom you are persecuting," the Lord replied. "Now get up and stand on your feet. I have appeared to you to appoint you as a servant and as a witness of what you have seen and will see of me. I will rescue you from your own people and from the Gentiles. I am sending you to them to open their eyes and turn them from darkness to light, and from the power of Satan to God, so that they may receive forgiveness of sins and a place among those who are sanctified by faith in me."'

ACTS 26:9–18 (TNIV)

In my experience, one of the most difficult things to accept about being a Christian is that, God being God, the place where I am and the things that are happening to me must be the best arrangements possible in my particular circumstances. Of course, if I am being deliberately rebellious or chronically disobedient, that may not be the case. But you know what I mean, don't you? God loves me. God wants the best for me. God organizes whatever is good for me. What else can I say? He is omnipotent. He is in charge.

Having said that, there is a sense in which I find it impossible to believe my own argument. There is something disturbingly unJesus-like and non-human (a tautology, of course) about the concept of living in this world as though nothing can alter unless God ordains or initiates the change. Jesus himself certainly wanted to be where the Father wanted him to be, and to do what the Father wanted him to do, but that total commitment never absolved him from the responsibility for making choices and actively pursuing his own initiatives. That's OK. It's just one more of those wonderfully creative tensions that characterize Christian experience and successfully thwart our desperate attempts to find simplistic answers to difficult questions.

So why am I airing my stumbling mental processes in this area? Well, it's all connected with these verses from Acts about Paul's amazing conversion. Some of the most significant blind spots are embodied in the most familiar passages, and this is a very good example. The question that I would like to ask, but never quite have, is this: 'Why not let everyone have a Damascus Road moment? Why not let me have one?'

I hope you will not misunderstand me when I say that I quite envy Paul this experience. I know that envy is a sin, but I'll repent after I've told you what I mean. I suppose it's just that Paul had such a very clear call to ministry. After more or less ambushing him on the road to Damascus, Jesus sets out the immensely significant job that lies before Saul, who is to become Paul, leaving him in no doubt about the reality and the value of their encounter.

Have you ever said to yourself that if God were to appear visibly before you and give you some hint of what the future holds, you know you would be able to go out and really work and evangelize for him? I have felt like that quite often since I became a follower of Jesus. Why doesn't he do it for hundreds of thousands of people whose lives would surely be revolutionized and changed for ever? After all, it seems to make perfect sense, doesn't it? All our doubts swept away by one unequivocal encounter with God.

Somehow, I honestly don't think so. I have a feeling that the growth of faith in things unseen has a much more enriching and substantiating effect on our lives as Christians than we can possibly imagine. Don't ask me how the spiritual mechanics of this argument operate, but when Jesus met the disciples after his resurrection, he said that those future followers who would believe without seeing are truly blessed (John 20:29). That means you and me. Perhaps, unlikely as it seems to our limited logical processes, we are more fortunate than Paul. And, in any case, I am sure you will agree with me that God does allow us refreshing glimpses and hints of his Aslan-like presence from time to time. Sometimes it doesn't feel like enough, but I suspect that it probably is.

A prayer

Father, some things we have to take on trust, and this is one of them. If you knew that vivid visual experiences of Jesus would be truly helpful to us, then I know that you would provide them. Help us to appreciate the privilege of being followers who have believed without seeing. Some day we shall understand such things, and in the meantime we will do our best to trust you. Oh, and I nearly forgot, I repent of my envy.

✣

A MATTER OF FOCUS

Now listen, you who say, 'Today or tomorrow we will go to this or that city, spend a year there, carry on business and make money.' Why, you do not even know what will happen tomorrow. What is your life? You are a mist that appears for a little while and then vanishes. Instead, you ought to say, 'If it is the Lord's will, we will live and do this or that.' As it is, you boast and brag. All such boasting is evil. So, then, if you know the good you ought to do and don't do it, you sin.
JAMES 4:13–17

If ever a passage was likely to put a spanner in the works of Western modern-day life, this is it. Talk about a deliberate blind spot! The idea that our important decisions about business and property and relocation should be dependent on the will of God goes sharply against the grain for many people.

As I write, the last of our children has left home and Bridget and I have the house to ourselves. The prospect is alarming and exciting. The children have been a huge part of our lives. We worked out years ago that if they all left home when they were 18, we would have had them for 30 years. Now that is what I call a long-term project! The reality of not having even one here is rather unnerving. It is just us, a dog called Lucy and a cat called Pepsi.

An exciting aspect of the situation is the realization that we could live anywhere we choose. All I need for my work is a place to plug my computer in, or a flat surface for a writing pad. It is pleasant to contemplate possibilities. Devon, Cornwall, North Yorkshire, Northumberland—what fun to go house-hunting in one or more of these beautiful counties. Or what about the New Forest? Green, mellow, restful.

I think it occurred to each of us at roughly the same time that, if our beliefs really mean anything, it cannot be a matter of simply picking a nice place to live and then moving there. God may be happy for us to live in one of those appealing locations, but, equally, he may not.

Twenty years ago, Bridget and I sat in the kitchen of the house we used to live in and told God that we wanted to go with him, to do something that would be of use to him, whatever might be involved and however inconvenient it might be for us. The series of events that occurred after our rash prayer suggests that God may have taken us at our word. It was as though our lives were turned upside down and shaken violently until they fell into the required shape. Out of the tumult of that time, a new career of writing and speaking began and, together with the raising of our family, that is what has been happening ever since. Now we seem to have arrived at a similar place of not knowing what the future does (or should) contain. Normally, couples of our age might be thinking of locating a place in which to settle for the rest of their years. Perhaps that is what we shall do, but we really are trying to be open to the most extreme or even bizarre requirements that God might have for our lives.

He may have a job for us to do in a place of his own choosing. It could be in England or in any other country in the world. I may continue to write, but only if it is part of his plan. We are trying to make a daily discipline out of placing the future in his hands, and opening our minds and spirits to any and every possibility. Not for one moment would I suggest that our hearts are completely committed to the proposition of total surrender yet, but at least we are now able to read this passage from James out of the corner of one eye.

There are disciplines involved in this process. The things that appear important to Bridget and me as we contemplate our future may be trivial in the context of God's plans for us. He has his own very specific way of focusing on aspects of this world. Learning to share and appreciate that focus requires real concentration. Every now and then, he has been teaching us a lesson. Let me give you a recent example.

One Wednesday afternoon, for instance, I found myself sitting in the front passenger seat of a mini-cab that had arrived to take me from the Goldhawk Road area of London to Victoria Station. I had been recording a radio play for an American Christian organization called *Focus on the Family*. I do moan about my life a little sometimes, but not very often, because I know how lucky I am to have so many different things to do. Travelling and speaking and writing and broadcasting and these odd bits of acting have provided me with exactly the kind of bits-and-pieces lifestyle that I dreamed of when I was younger.

As my cab pulled out on to Goldhawk Road, I reflected on the fact that taking part in these radio plays has been a relatively recent addition to my activities, bringing me full circle to my earliest and most passionate dream of being an actor. The first play in the series that we recorded had been a disaster as far as I was concerned. I was rubbish. But earlier that day, as we were completing our sixth recording in about three years, I had realized that I was feeling much more confident. And it was fun meeting with 'real' actors—the more obscure, younger ones as well as the odd household name.

As we turned into one of those delightfully leafy streets that pop up unexpectedly in every part of our great capital city, I quizzed myself over what God might think of all these different activities of mine. 'Show me Jesus in it all, so that I can follow him,' I asked, a little pompously. I suspect I was feeling rather pleased with myself.

My musings were interrupted by the young cab driver, who asked me where I would be travelling to after he dropped me off at Victoria. I told him that my home was in the market town of Hailsham, a few miles north of Eastbourne—one of the sunniest places in Great Britain, for what it was worth. He told me he had been to Eastbourne on holiday as a child and remembered liking it very much. He wanted to know what I did for a living. I told him that I was mainly a writer, but that I sometimes did other things as well.

'What about you?' I asked. 'Tell me about yourself.'

My new friend was a third-generation British West Indian. He had a wife and a new baby and he was intensely proud of both. At present, they were living in a one-bedroom flat in the north of London, but he was worried that when the baby got bigger the family would need larger accommodation. Prices being what they were, he couldn't see how this would be possible. He worked very long hours in his taxi, earning as much as he could to support his family. Sometimes, he told me rather ruefully, he was at home for only a few hours in the week. He would dearly love to move right out of London, to a place like Eastbourne, in fact. He was well aware, though, that such a move would not be possible in the foreseeable future.

All the way to Victoria, my driver continued to talk with bright animation about the hopes and concerns and passions that filled each day of his life. Once or twice, when something struck him with extra force, he smacked the steering wheel lightly with one hand.

Eventually he dropped me at the back entrance to Victoria Station and pulled away in the direction of his next job with a cheery wave of the hand. I stood on the pavement for a moment, my suitcase in my hand, considering the conclusion I had reached through listening to this young man for the last 20 minutes. It was something about vision—something about the way in which Jesus sees the world, as opposed to my own perspective.

'That encounter was the most useful and important thing that will happen to you today,' said the one who still walks this world looking for small adventures with large consequences, seeing the events and people that really count, and bypassing the superficial preoccupations of a deluded world.

As I have already said, it is a matter of focus, and, for me or anyone else, the adjustment requires a great deal of obedience and practice. Bridget and I are praying that, whatever the future brings, we get it right.

A prayer

Father, it can hurt to stay within your will. It is very tempting to pursue those goals that appear to offer us personal ease and comfort. After all, that's what most normal people do. In our hearts, though, Father, we do want to be at the centre of the plan you have for us. Help us to be strong and obedient, both for your sake and for ours. Forgive our selfishness and show us where our real priorities lie. May we never judge significance by the world's standards. We want to share your focus, to see situations and people as you see them. Thank you for the lessons you teach us, Lord.

---- ✜ ----

A FATHER'S HEART

Every year Jesus' parents went to Jerusalem for the Feast of the Passover. When he was twelve years old, they went up to the Feast, according to the custom. After the Feast was over, while his parents were returning home, the boy Jesus stayed behind in Jerusalem, but they were unaware of it. Thinking he was in their company, they travelled on for a day. Then they began looking for him among their relatives and friends. When they did not find him, they went back to Jerusalem to look for him. After three days they found him in the temple courts, sitting among the teachers, listening to them and asking questions. Everyone who heard him was amazed at his understanding and his answers. When his parents saw him, they were astonished. His mother said to him, 'Son, why have you treated us like this? Your father and I have been anxiously searching for you.'

'Why were you searching for me?' he asked. 'Didn't you know I had to be in my Father's house?' But they did not understand what he was saying to them.

Then he went down to Nazareth with them and was obedient to them.

But his mother treasured all these things in her heart. And as Jesus grew up, he increased in wisdom and in favour with God and people.
LUKE 2:41–52 (TNIV)

There is something very sad here.

I don't know what sort of person Joseph was, although I think it is fair to assume that he would never have been selected and allowed to undertake the earthly parenting of Jesus if he had not been the sort of man who would make a good father. What does that mean? Well, I suppose it implies a combination of firmness and flexibility, a willingness to laugh and play at appropriate times, and a certain steadiness of approach to life, the kind of consistency that a growing boy needs. Above all, he would be someone capable of feeling, expressing and receiving love, and therefore he must have been as vulnerable as the rest of us are in our relationships. Love is always a risk. If you love, you can be hurt. Those are the rules. They affect us. They affect God. They will never change.

Joseph brought Jesus up as his own, and probably loved him as much as if he had been his natural son. You don't search anxiously for someone who means nothing to you.

How did this good man react to the statement Jesus made about having to be in his Father's house? Apart from anything else, we are told that neither Joseph nor Mary had the slightest idea what the boy was talking about. This might seem a little puzzling when you consider that both of them were well aware of something very special and very different about their son. All those angel visits and dreams in the distant past—might they not have made some kind of connection?

On the other hand, twelve years is quite a long time in the life of a family, long enough perhaps for those memories to seem like a distant dream with no practical bearing on the present. There may even have been an element of denial in Mary's response. Why would she wish to hasten the piercing of her heart with that prophesied sword of sorrow? Until we are able to ask Mary face to face, we can only speculate on these things.

53

Here is another speculation, just for good measure, and this is the sad thought that afflicted me when I read this passage for the thousandth time. I asked myself if, for one confused and emotionally swirling moment, Joseph might have wondered how the boy could be confusing the carpentry workshop back home with the temple courts of Jerusalem. How could he possibly have mistaken this grand and sacred building for his father's humble dwelling in Nazareth?

Did the truth strike him quite suddenly then, or was it much later? And did that truth feel like his own very particular and excruciating sword in the heart? In front of his eyes, that distant, angel-inhabited past had rushed like a whirlwind to catch up with and overtake the present. Of course, of course! The young, self-assured Jesus was not talking about the man who had so willingly loved and cared for him since the day of his birth. He was not talking about his adoptive father at all. He was talking about his real father. He was talking about God. And with that realization, life, for Joseph at least, was surely never quite the same again.

A prayer

Thank you, Father, for the sacrificial lives of your good servants across the years. Joseph played a crucial role in the great salvation plan, and we salute him for his willing obedience. May we also be able to step back when our role in any task is finished, and allow others to take it to completion.

YOUR MONEY OR YOUR LIFE

Now a man named Ananias, together with his wife Sapphira, also sold a piece of property. With his wife's full knowledge he kept back part of the money for himself, but brought the rest and put it at the apostles' feet.

Then Peter said, 'Ananias, how is it that Satan has so filled your heart that you have lied to the Holy Spirit and have kept for yourself some of the money you received for the land? Didn't it belong to you before it was sold? And after it was sold, wasn't the money at your disposal? What made you think of doing such a thing? You have not lied to men but to God.

When Ananias heard this, he fell down and died.

ACTS 5:1–5

A blind spot? Not in one sense. The tale is well known. This devious couple lied to the apostles and, by inference, to the Holy Spirit. Result? They dropped dead. Dramatic, shocking and salutary. Heavy-duty logic.

There is a blind spot, though. Someone once wrote asking why I thought such a heavy penalty was imposed by God because of one lie. I realized that the same question has lodged somewhere in my mind since I first read Acts. Why such severity? They brought half the money. Did that not count?

The obvious question is: why did the couple decide to lie about their gift? As Peter said, they didn't have to give anything. They could have kept their property, or brought half the money and been honest about keeping the rest. That would have been fine. Why the lie? Was it actually an issue of faith, or lack of faith? Were Ananias and Sapphira trying to keep a foot in both camps? If the Christian thing turned out to be a load of rubbish—well, it wouldn't matter because they had half the cash stashed away. If it was true, then they had made a significant financial investment into their spiritual future by appearing to give the whole amount.

If they truly were capable of thinking in such a way, then they had not even begun to genuinely understand the Christian faith. Was their punishment so severe because they had hedged their bets? I don't know, but I have an uneasy idea that I might have the same problem, less with my money than with my commitment, and I say this because I know how difficult I have found it to be faithful and generous to God in relatively small matters.

A memory surfaces—one of those memories that fills my face with a hot tide of shame. I was in a car with a friend. He was not a Christian, but he was, if I may put it like this, a very good friend of the family, and I had known him since long before I became a believer. He was driving. (He would have to have been, because I never did learn to do it and never will, unless God puts his foot down—if you see what I mean.) We were enjoying a trip through the Kent countryside. The air was fresh and full of the soft, deliriously intoxicating scent of an early English summer. The plan was to end up at some convivial establishment for an outdoor lunch. What more could one want in this world?

As we journeyed, we talked about all sorts of pleasant, trivial things. Eventually, we got on to the subject of mutual acquaintances. My friend mentioned a man who may or may not be called George. We talked about where each of us met George, and reminded ourselves of things we had done together in the past. At a certain point in the dialogue, I remembered something about this absent friend that was intensely private and certainly not for sharing, but would make a very funny story. I conducted a short inward debate.

'Look,' I said to myself, 'it's not as if the man sitting next to me is going to pass this information on to anyone else. He's a friend. I can tell him it's strictly in confidence. I know I can trust him. And it does make such a very funny story. Let's face it, he and I and George laugh at each other all the time anyway. George wouldn't mind. Go on! Tell the story.'

I opened my mouth. A hand landed on my shoulder.

'Don't tell the story.'

'But it's so funny!'

'Don't tell the story.'

'But he wouldn't mind. And I know I can trust my friend.'

'Like George trusted you? Don't tell the story.'

'Oh, but I can make it so very funny! So very *very* funny.'

Silence.

I didn't tell the story.

I broke out in a bit of a cold sweat. I had come razor-thin close to letting my friend George down very badly. It was like a fever, a mini-madness. All for the sake of a laugh. A bowl of soup. The wrong woman. Half the price of a field. Thirty pieces of silver.

A prayer

Father, if there is a bet-hedging fault in us, reveal it and forgive us. It is true that there are times when greed or pride or some other appetite distracts us from the clear path of commitment and truth. And help us to guard our tongues, Lord. Sometimes the gift we need to offer you is nothing more or less than our silence and discretion. Thank you for forgiving us for failures in the past and for allowing us to start again.

———————— ❖ ————————

BUY ONE, GET ONE FREE?

Jesus entered Jericho and was passing through. A man was there by the name of Zacchaeus; he was a chief tax collector and was wealthy. He wanted to see who Jesus was, but because he was short he could not see over the crowd. So he ran ahead and climbed a sycomore-fig tree to see him, since Jesus was coming that way.

When Jesus reached the spot, he looked up and said to him, 'Zacchaeus, come down immediately. I must stay at your house today.' So he came down at once and welcomed him gladly.

All the people saw this and began to mutter, 'He has gone to be the guest of a "sinner".'

But Zacchaeus stood up and said to the Lord, 'Look, Lord! Here and now I give half of my possessions to the poor, and if I have cheated anyone out of anything, I will pay back four times the amount.'

Jesus said to him, 'Today salvation has come to this house, because this man, too, is a son of Abraham. For the Son of Man came to seek and to save what was lost.'

LUKE 19:1–10 (TNIV)

As Jesus started on his way, a man ran up to him and fell on his knees before him. 'Good teacher,' he asked, 'what must I do to inherit eternal life?'

'Why do you call me good?' Jesus answered. 'No-one is good—except God alone. You know the commandments: "You shall not murder, you shall not commit adultery, you shall not steal, you shall not give false testimony, you shall not defraud, honour your father and mother."'

'Teacher,' he declared, 'all these have I kept since I was a boy.'

Jesus looked at him and loved him. 'One thing you lack,' he said. 'Go, sell everything you have and give to the poor, and you will have treasure in heaven. Then come, follow me.'

At this the man's face fell. He went away sad, because he had great wealth.

MARK 10:17–22 (TNIV)

OK, so let us imagine that Zacchaeus and the rich young man meet up at some later date and compare notes.

'You might be interested to hear,' says Zacchaeus, 'about an encounter I had with that teacher called Jesus. It was fantastic! He just suddenly announced that he was coming to tea at my house. I was up a tree at the time, and—'

'Up a tree?'

'Yes, up a tree, it doesn't matter why, and it was as though everything sort of fell into place on the spot. He called me down, we had a great meal, and I told him and everyone else who was there that I was going to give away half of all my stuff to the poor and pay back four times what I owed to anyone I'd cheated. And do you know what he said? He said—'

'Sorry, how much did you tell him you were going to give away?' interrupts the other man, clearly extremely interested.

'Half of all I possessed,' replies Zacchaeus with slight impatience, 'but do you want to hear what he said?'

'Oh, yes. I do. I really do. Sorry—go on.'

The whole of the small being that is Zacchaeus seems to expand and beam with the memory. 'He said that salvation had come to my house, and he more or less implied that I had been lost, but that now I was saved. Wonderful. He's not just a teacher, you know. I believe he's the Son of God.'

'And did you do all those things you promised? Have you stuck to it?'

'Oh, yes. I certainly did. I have. I never want to go back to being the rat I was before he came along. I was horrible.' A little shudder passes through him. 'I was *so* unpleasant.'

There is a pause before the rich man speaks again. The expression on his face is one of mingled sadness and perplexity.

'I met him once as well, you know. I wanted what you seem to have been given. I wanted it *so* much. I wanted to be saved, to know that I would live for ever.' A hollow laugh escapes him. 'I was really confident, too. Embarrassingly so. You say you used to be a rat— you probably weren't as bad as you thought you were—'

'Oh yes I was. Worse, probably. Rat cubed.'

'Anyway, what I was going to say was that, although I was never perfect, I really had tried all my life to get things right, ever since I was a boy. It's how I was brought up. I honestly had done my best. I worked hard at being good. But there was still this nagging worry in me that when it came to the crunch, whatever the crunch turned out to be, I'd disappear into the darkness and just be lost. And this teacher, this Jesus, somehow seemed to have the power or the authority to sort it out for me. I agree with you. I think he was the Son of God as well. But…'

'What happened?'

'Well, he did listen to what I said. He was very nice to me, actually. I got the impression that he genuinely liked me. But in the end—the thing he asked me to do—I don't know, I just couldn't bring myself even to think of going along with it.'

'And what was it he wanted you to do?'

The rich man sighs, perhaps contemplating a memory that refuses to change or fade with the years.

'He wanted me to sell up. Sell everything I'd got and give the proceeds to the poor. Every single thing. After that, I think the idea was that I would just follow him.'

'Like what happened to me, then,' suggests Zacchaeus brightly.

'No, no!' The other man shakes his head in brisk disagreement. 'No, with all due respect, it's not the same as what happened to you. You gave away half of what you owned, but you kept the other half—'

'Well, I did need quite a bit of that for the paying back four times thing, and—'

'And he told you that salvation had come to your house, and that you were saved. He gave you the thing I wanted so much but at only half the cost. So, what was that, an unrepeatable special offer or something? Buy one, get one free? How can that be fair? You tell me. How can that be right?'

Zacchaeus shifts a little uncomfortably in his seat, uncertain how to answer.

'I actually did want to change deep inside,' the little man says haltingly at last. 'I was sick with myself. Sick with my own greed and unkindness. I didn't want to be that person, but... well, without making excuses, the sheer momentum of it all just kept on carrying me along. Then Jesus turned up and I suppose I thought this might be someone who could, well, give me permission to come out of the tiny cave that the best part of me always seemed to be crouching in. That's why I followed him through the crowds that day. I climbed the tree because—' He clears his throat self-consciously. 'I climbed the tree because, as you can see, I am at the higher end of the not-significantly-tall range, and I knew I'd never be able to see him over all those bodies and heads.

'Oh, it was such a joy and a... a relief when he stopped and called up to me. To me! So exciting! In fact, for the first time in years, I felt like dancing. I mean, I didn't. It's not a good idea to dance when you're sitting in the top of a tree, nor when you're climbing down one, but if it was, then I would have… if you see what I mean.'

He pauses, choosing his words carefully. 'You know, I think if he had asked me to sell or give away every single bit of what I had, then I probably would have done. Not because I was a better person than you. That's silly. Obviously I wasn't. But what I wanted more than anything was to be what he wanted me to be, and I have to tell you that after that day I felt so clean, and so… so very rich. I still am. So *rich*.'

He pauses once more before continuing softly. 'So, why—you know—why couldn't you do what he asked?'

'Frightened,' replies the rich man sadly. 'I figured he was asking me to stop being me. It wasn't really the money in itself. I know that now. You're going to think this sounds silly, but I don't think I've quite understood what was going on, not until hearing what you've just been saying to me. In my own mind I was—what would the word be?—I was *defined* by my wealth. I couldn't see what or who I would end up being if I just let it all drop away from me like a cloak.'

He stares into the distance for a moment. 'I didn't think anyone would like me without my cloak. I think I wanted eternal life in return for being good. I wanted… *it*. I didn't want him. Now I do. Do you think he might still be interested?'

'Still interested? Oh, yes. Sure of it.' Zacchaeus nods earnestly. 'I'm absolutely sure of it.'

A prayer

Lord Jesus, it is so very hard for us to find the source of our true wealth in you. Fragile beings we are, and so insecure when we take faltering steps outside an identity that is meaningful only in the eyes of the world. We know that it is not about money, Lord, but about our willingness to offer you freely anything that occupies the central place in our lives and therefore excludes you. Give us honesty and courage in our consideration of this matter, Lord Jesus. Thank you for giving us cause to dance in our trees.

WHAT IS TRUTH?

When the Jewish Feast of Tabernacles was near, Jesus' brothers said to him, 'You ought to leave here and go to Judea, so that your disciples may see the miracles you do. No one who wants to become a public figure acts in secret. Since you are doing these things, show yourself to the world.' For even his own brothers did not believe in him.

Therefore Jesus told them, 'The right time for me has not come; for you any time is right. The world cannot hate you, but it hates me because I testify that what it does is evil. You go to the Feast. I am not yet going up to this Feast, because for me the right time has not yet come.' Having said this, he stayed in Galilee.

However, after his brothers had left for the Feast, he went also, not publicly but in secret.

JOHN 7:2–10

Did these brothers honestly suppose that their footling argument would affect Jesus' plans? The absurd suggestion that he was motivated by a desire to become a public figure shows how distanced they were from the truth. Some people, Christians included, suffer from the same confusion in this age. Celebrity is seductive.

In fact, what those rotten, unbelieving brothers of his were trying to do was very unpleasant. They knew how dangerous it would be for him to travel openly. Were they hoping that their brother's death would remove the embarrassment they had suffered as a result of his singular activities? Whatever their motivation, Jesus saw through it, as he saw and sees through all dodgy motivation. 'You go ahead,' he told them. 'It's dangerous for me. I'm staying here in Galilee.'

But he *didn't*, did he?

As soon as they'd gone, he set off for the feast secretly, divinely incognito, to coin a phrase.

Here, then, is my question about this particular blind spot. Was it all right for Jesus to shade the truth as he clearly did in telling his brothers he wasn't going to the feast yet?

Let's just take a look at this question of telling the truth for a moment. More specifically, let me ask myself if there are times when I am less than truthful, and, if there are such times, is my lack of straightforwardness on those occasions ever justified? Several things immediately spring to mind. How about you? I shall share two or three of my thoughts with you. Not all—just two or three.

First, I have a daughter. Kate is 18 as I write, and away at university. On various occasions over the years in which Kate and I have lived in the same house, my opinion has been solicited concerning the effect or suitability of a dress or a skirt or a top or a pair of shoes or a scarf or a style of make-up. What does it look like? Is it all right? Am I overdressed? Am I underdressed? Do they, or does it, go with my hair? Speaking of my hair, is it all right? Should it be down? Or up? How's my fringe?

Leaving aside for the moment the fact that I am less qualified to make judgments in such matters than just about everyone else in the entire universe, these questions can be extremely difficult to answer truthfully.

Picture, for instance, one of those Friday evenings when Kate was 15 or 16. It is eight o'clock and she has spent the last four or five hours tensely and meticulously preparing herself for one of those crucial social events, the failure of which will, in her mind at least, blight any chance of happiness she might have had for the whole of the rest of her life. Finally, with only minutes to spare before being picked up, she emerges from her bedroom, descends the stairs and presents herself worriedly in the doorway of the sitting-room, balanced like an over-filled glass of water that is about to spill everywhere.

'Do I look all right?'

Now this, as all parents of teenagers will tell you, is not a question. It may have an interrogation mark at the end of itself, and it may be delivered with the rising inflection that commonly characterizes a query, but it is not a question. It is a direct plea for reassurance. If it was an item in a multi-choice exam, there would only be one little box available to tick, and that little box would be next to the legend, 'You look absolutely great!'

I suppose I could have stuck to the letter of the law. I could have said, 'Darling, I realize that your lift will be here in a couple of minutes, but, as a Christian, I do feel that I am obliged to answer your question with complete accuracy. Our Lord tells us in the eighth chapter of John's Gospel that the truth will set us free, and that is what I am going to do for you now. So, bearing that in mind, I think your skirt is too short, your top is too revealing, you've got too much eyeshadow on and the colour of your bag is too near the colour of your coat and too different from the colour of your boots to work with either. Have a lovely evening, sweetheart.'

Truth and kindness are charmingly courteous to each other. They take turns making way.

A second scenario—a slightly more tricky one this time. I am slumped on a chair in the kitchen just after getting up in the morning. My wife is doing something with marmalade. The phone rings in the study. Bridget disappears to pick it up and reappears in the kitchen after a few seconds, mouthing the name of the person on the other end as she walks through the door. I shrink, as far as I am able, into the corner of my chair. Please! Not at this time of the morning. Not this particular person. Not now. Bridget and I embark on a totally silent but furiously intense conversation.

'He wants to speak to you!' mouths Bridget, her lips forming the words with wildly exaggerated precision. 'Are you in?'

'No,' I mouth back frantically, shaking my hands from the wrists rapidly and defensively in front of me, 'I'm not here! Say I'm not here!'

'But he wants to speak to you!'

'I don't care! I'm not here! I'll phone him later!'

'You'll *what*?'

'I'll phone him LATER. L-A-A-A-T-E-E-E-R!'

Abruptly, a miraculous change occurs in Bridget's manner. Her whole face relaxes and her voice, as she speaks into the phone, is a fluting symphony of concern and regret. 'I'm terribly sorry, but he's not actually here at the moment. I'll tell him you called as soon as he comes in and he'll phone you straight back...'

I hasten to add that the same thing happens the other way round with equal frequency. It is a lie, isn't it? I suppose husbands and wives get into the habit of covering for each other in this sort of way. Is it OK? Is it a terrible sin? What do you think?

On the other side of this particular coin are those occasions when someone really does desperately need to talk things through and, halfway through the conversation, will break off nervously and say, 'Look, you don't want to hear me going on and on about myself. You must be tired. Do you want me to go?'

Well, you might be tired, and there might be a part of you that would love to be left in peace to watch something stupid on television, but there is a greater and much more important truth that overrides mere factual accuracy. 'No,' you reply, 'don't worry. I'm fine. Go on with what you were saying.' You are certainly not going to say, 'Yes, that is true. I don't particularly want to hear any more about your troubles. I am tired, and *The Bill* is about to start. So, all things considered, it would be good if you could go now.'

People have been kind enough to avoid saying that to me once or twice in the past, and I am very grateful to them.

Honesty compels me to add that there are also times, usually when I feel cornered or threatened, when I tell glaring, deliberate lies. Thank God, that doesn't happen very much any more, but when it does I feel deeply ashamed.

All in all, though, as we have seen, this question of telling the truth is very far from being a black-and-white one. I don't know your answer to that question about whether it was all right for Jesus to shade the truth, but I don't think it really matters. As I have already said, there is a truth that is greater than accuracy. Jesus was not imprisoned by rules but empowered by love, as we should be. God grant us discernment.

A prayer

Father, we would rather have your vision than our own of what is needed and what is not, of what is right and what is wrong. We pray that in all things we shall be motivated by a desire to please you, and not by selfishness or laziness. Forgive the deliberate dishonesty we have been guilty of and help us to be wise in our role as guardians of truth and kindness.

BEYOND THE VEIL

---— ✤ ———

LUSTFUL ANGELS AND WAR IN HEAVEN: THE HARD QUESTIONS

When human beings began to increase in number on the earth and daughters were born to them, the sons of God saw that these daughters were beautiful, and they married any of them they chose. Then the Lord said, 'My Spirit will not contend with human beings forever, for they are mortal; their days will be a hundred and twenty years.'

The Nephilim were on the earth in those days—and also afterwards—when the sons of God went to the daughters of the human beings and had children by them. They were the heroes of old, men of renown.

The Lord saw how great the wickedness of the human race had become on the earth, and that every inclination of the thoughts of the human heart was only evil all the time. The Lord regretted that he had made human beings on the earth, and his heart was deeply troubled. So the Lord said, 'I will wipe from the face of the earth the human race I have created—and with them the animals, the birds and the creatures that move along the ground—for I regret that I have made them.' But Noah found favour in the eyes of the Lord.

GENESIS 6:1–8 (TNIV)

For if God did not spare angels when they sinned, but sent them to hell, putting them into gloomy dungeons to be held for judgment...

2 PETER 2:4

And the angels who did not keep their positions of authority but abandoned their proper dwelling—these he has kept in darkness, bound with everlasting chains for judgment on the great Day.

JUDE 6 (TNIV)

OK, time to rush around collecting concordances and commentaries and biblical encyclopedias and anything else that might help. What on earth or anywhere else is this about? It's all rather reminiscent of that man with a Dutch-sounding name who wrote those very unconvincing books in the 1960s, claiming that the human race was visited by beings from outer space in the distant past. His treatises were full of sentences beginning with such phrases as 'There is little doubt that…' or 'Surely it is reasonable to assume…' or 'Can anyone seriously dispute the proposition…'. Quite entertaining, but bizarre and nonsensical.

In fact, according to what we read here, the truth, if that is what it is, may be stranger still. The consensus appears to be that these passages are talking about angels who, against the will of God, abandoned their authority and left the heavenly regions in order to marry the beautiful daughters of men. As a consequence, they were imprisoned in gloomy caverns where they are still awaiting judgment on, as Jude puts it, the great Day. This misbehaviour on the part of the angels, coupled with the general sinfulness of humanity, was the reason for God's decision to flood the world and destroy everyone except Noah and his family.

All right, what are we to do with this extraordinary information? If we decide to believe it unreservedly, some very uncomfortable questions are thrown up. They are not really new questions, because they apply equally to the whole question of Satan. Have a look at this truly remarkable passage from the book of Revelation:

And there was war in heaven. Michael and his angels fought against the dragon, and the dragon and his angels fought back. But he was not strong enough, and they lost their place in heaven. The great dragon was hurled down—that ancient snake called the devil, or Satan, who leads the whole world astray. He was hurled to the earth, and his angels with him. Then I heard a loud voice say:

'Now have come the salvation and the power and the kingdom of our God, and the authority of his Messiah. For the accuser of our brothers and sisters, who accuses them before our God day and night, has been hurled

down. They triumphed over him by the blood of the Lamb and by the word
of their testimony; they did not love their lives so much as to shrink from
death. Therefore rejoice, you heavens and you who dwell in them! But woe
to the earth and the sea, because the devil has gone down to you! He is
filled with fury, because he knows that his time is short.'
REVELATION 12:7–12 (TNIV)

Those questions I mentioned just now have never got any more comfortable over the years. Let us bluntly ask ourselves a really obvious one. Why would these angels, these Nephilim, who actually lived in heaven, consider a fling with a human being, however beautiful, preferable to remaining in the presence of God? Why would they? And if the devil really is a fallen angel, why did he fall? How could he fall? Are we to believe that he became bored, or discontented, or disillusioned with the way things were in the golden city? Does that make any sense at all?

Over the last few years, I have become increasingly warmed up to the prospect of seeing heaven for myself, and, like many others, I have automatically assumed that it will turn out to be a place where things can never go wrong because God is in charge and all manner of things will be perfectly well. The initial impression left on me by these passages, however, is markedly different. They make heaven sound rather like one of those neighbourhoods where the police are constantly being called because voices are raised and furniture is thrown around and fighting has broken out. All in all, it sounds a lot more unstable and poorly controlled than one might have imagined or hoped for.

A further question. Is it possible that I too might become disenchanted with the Creator after a few millennia in paradise, and seek to establish my own little faction in opposition to his authority? It sounds ridiculous, and I most sincerely hope it is, but hard questions are not going to evaporate and blow away just because I don't like them.

Some will say, 'Hold on a minute. I understand perfectly what you're getting at, but what you have to understand is that this is just picture language. There was no actual battle in heaven. Nobody literally fell from anywhere. And the Nephilim are basically symbols of evil entering the hearts of men and women—a moral truth as opposed to a factual one. It's a sort of teaching aid, you see.'

Well, I might go along with that idea (I certainly do and have done in connection with other 'difficult' bits of the Bible) if it weren't for two things. The first is the extract from Peter's second letter that I have already quoted. Peter was very close to Jesus and his pronouncements after Pentecost seem to have been exclusively inspired by the Holy Spirit. I am very impressed that Peter speaks of these same erring angels in a way that suggests they really do exist, and that they really are imprisoned in those dark and gloomy caverns.

The other thing is that Jesus himself mentions the fall of Satan in the tenth chapter of Luke's Gospel, just after his 72 newly trained disciples return, flushed with success from their first ministry expedition.

The seventy-two returned with joy and said, 'Lord, even the demons submit to us in your name.'

He replied, 'I saw Satan fall like lightning from heaven. I have given you authority to trample on snakes and scorpions and to overcome all the power of the enemy; nothing will harm you. However, do not rejoice that the spirits submit to you, but rejoice that your names are written in heaven.'

At that time Jesus, full of joy through the Holy Spirit, said, 'I praise you, Father, Lord of heaven and earth, because you have hidden these things from the wise and learned, and revealed them to little children. Yes, Father, for this was your good pleasure.'

LUKE 10:17–21

Time is fluid in the world of the spirit. Filled with an unspeakable joy, Jesus sees Satan fall from heaven after his defeat, with a flash of lightning that floods and flushes the darkness out of eternity. In that moment he knows that the war is won, even if some desperately bloody battles remain to be fought.

So, no, for these reasons I cannot quite bring myself to accept that these are nothing but instructive pictures, and I have yet another reason for not regarding them in such a way. You see, there is a sense in which I find these extraordinary stories and references, if true, genuinely helpful. Before I explain why that is, have a look at this passage from the tenth chapter of the book of Daniel. After mourning and fasting for three weeks, Daniel is standing on the banks of the Tigris when an amazing figure with a face like lightning, eyes like flaming torches and a voice like multitudes appears before him and speaks the following words.

Do not be afraid, Daniel. Since the first day that you set your mind to gain understanding and to humble yourself before your God, your words were heard, and I have come in response to them. But the prince of the Persian kingdom resisted me twenty-one days. Then Michael, one of the chief princes, came to help me, because I was detained there with the king of Persia (vv. 12–13).

Now, I have only the haziest notion of the meaning of all this, but what it conveys to me is an intriguing sense of dramatic activity in a sphere of existence that is commonly hidden from human eyes. Real *Lord of the Rings* stuff.

Put it all together and what have we got? War in heaven. Satan falling like lightning, banished to the earth. Rebellious angels imprisoned in underground caverns. The archangel Michael lending his weight to a mystery man who is battling to get through to Daniel.

These and other biblical references suggest, with quite startling vividness, that the spiritual realm is one of conflict, urgency and upheaval, of possible failure and incipient triumph. They portray a place where most of the really important battles are fought and, thanks to Jesus, won by the right side. Why do I find this helpful? Because in this context so many more things make sense, or at least have the potential for making sense. As we have already said, there are so many difficult questions, and they cannot be briskly swept under the carpet, especially as they are the questions that are continually asked by people who are not Christians. Here are a few more of them.

Why did God create a world, knowing that it would fall and that, as a consequence, his Son was bound to suffer unspeakably as a result? Did God really, as recorded in Genesis, 'regret' that he had created men and women?

If it comes to that, why did Jesus have to come to earth at all? An all-powerful God is surely able to choose from as many options for problem-solving as he wishes.

What is the point of so much intense suffering for so many people? Three little boys suffocate in a freezer that has been dumped in a wood. Did God see that happening? Why did he not stop it? A little girl in the slums of Bangladesh becomes a prostitute at the age of six and dies at the age of eight. Why? Why did God not rescue her? Why do we have to be his hands and feet in this world? At Gethsemane, Jesus indicated to Simon Peter that there are legions of angels available. Why not use them?

Why is Satan allowed any power at all in the world? What is the point of permitting him to destroy the eternal lives of so many people, particularly as he is supposedly defeated? Why are there any concessions at all to the devil? Bound for a thousand years and then set free for a short time? Why the short time? Why not get rid of him immediately and altogether and move straight to the new heaven and the new earth?

I probably know and have supplied most of the statutory answers to these questions, but I have never found any of them very satis-fying. Nowadays, I make no attempt to pretend otherwise. I have no doubt that God does not in any sense wish to be 'let off the hook'. This makes explanations difficult, to say the very least, but in the context of such questions there are three things I can definitely say to enquirers.

The first is that my faith begins and ends with Jesus, and I obediently trust that he holds answers and solutions to all my most difficult questions and problems. He is the hub, the centre of my life, the person who, by his very existence, gives meaning to all things. If I never understand anything else, it will be enough that he knows me.

Second, given the things that have happened and are still happening, it is blatantly obvious that there are vast swathes of information about God, heaven, the world and the relationship between all three that we simply do not have, and would not properly understand if they were available to us.

Third, as I have already said, it seems clear from scripture that there is tumult and conflict behind the scenes, as it were, beyond anything that we could possibly imagine. We are bound to use logic in our deliberations—and we should do, because that is how our thinking about faith develops and moves forward—but we cannot be logical about something that can hardly be perceived at all from the perspective of ordinary human lives.

'The truth will set us free,' Jesus said. The truth is that I trust him, and because of that I will not produce half-baked answers in response to impossible questions. If he should care to supply me with explanations in these areas, I would be grateful. If not, then I can wait. It feels good to be free.

A prayer

Father, we are surrounded by mysteries. One day, when all things are revealed, we shall understand. In the meantime, thank you for what we do understand, and in particular for the knowledge that we are called to know and be known by Jesus, to serve you and others in this world and to enjoy freedom through commitment to the truth.

---------------- ❖ ----------------

THE UNDEAD—AND A
FASCINATING ENCOUNTER

At that moment the curtain of the temple was torn in two from top to bottom. The earth shook and the rocks split. The tombs broke open and the bodies of many holy people who had died were raised to life. They came out of the tombs, and after Jesus' resurrection they went into the holy city and appeared to many people.

MATTHEW 27:51–53

Well, here's a thing, then. It's like something out of one of those *Hammer Horror* movies where the 'undead' pursue the hero with stiff legs and empty eye-sockets. I never have found those films very convincing, have you? I am certainly not the first to ask this question, but why is it that slow-moving creatures like the undead and mummies and other rigid-jointed creatures of the night are able to catch human beings who are patently capable of moving several times faster than them? Puzzling, isn't it? Perhaps fear paralyses the victims. Forgive me. I digress. This is completely different—I hope.

What on earth is happening here? Apparently, many holy people came to life when their tombs split open, and they went into the city. Not just a few, but many. Did you gather that? They went into the city. Went into the city to do what? Did they look up old friends and family members? Must have been something of a shock for them, mustn't it—especially the younger ones.

'This is your Great-Uncle Nathaniel who we've told you about. Yes, that's right, he did die 30 years ago, but that's no reason for you not to be polite. And stop wrinkling your nose like that. You wouldn't smell very wonderful if you'd been in a tomb for three decades. You sit yourself down, Uncle Nat, and tell us what you've been up—or down to lately.'

Did little groups of resurrected holy men sit around in local taverns in their grave clothes, comparing notes over a flagon of wine, feeling more than a little bewildered and wishing there was a tour guide? What did they look like? And where did these singular individuals go in the end? Did they clamber miserably back into their tombs eventually, slamming the doors behind them, or did they live out the rest of their new lives with friends or relatives until they were overtaken by a second death? Who knows? I certainly don't.

What I do think I understand is that the death and triumph of Jesus on the cross abruptly, dramatically, fundamentally altered the rules that had hitherto applied to the business of living and dying. Now, there was to be a new fluidity of traffic between heaven and earth, material and spiritual—a new definition, in fact, of what it means to be alive. Read about Jesus after the resurrection, and then read Acts. See how it all started to work out. It's very exciting.

While we are on the subject of traffic flowing between heaven and earth, I would like to tell you about something that happened to me a few years ago. I was speaking in Dorset at a rather pretty church overlooking the ocean in a well-known seaside town. After the service, I positioned myself in the porch so that I could greet and shake hands with members of the congregation as they left. Towards the end of this pleasant process, a very old lady, in her 90s as I subsequently learned, approached me and reached her arms up to pull my head down so that she could kiss me on the cheek.

'Thank you so much for your talk,' she said. 'I really enjoyed it, especially when you spoke about being a writer.'

'Well, thank you,' I replied. 'I very much enjoyed being here. And thank you for coming.' I meant what I said, but it was very much a standard form of response.

'Yes,' she continued, 'I particularly appreciated the bit about your writing because my husband was a writer as well.'

'Really!' I simulated deep amazement at this staggering synchronicity. People often told me that they or their husbands or wives or uncles or aunts were writers. It could mean anything or nothing. It could mean that they had written half a book, or the first line of a book, or three whole books that had never been published, or the occasional magazine article, or, very occasionally, that they really were established authors.

'He wrote quite a lot of books,' said the neat little lady, a quiet smile of pride on her face, 'mostly about the Bible.'

I pictured a dusty study in which tediously inaccessible tomes were produced for a minority readership by some narrowly scholastic student of ancient languages.

'I see.' I fear that my tone was very slightly patronizing. 'And what was his name?'

'Phillips,' she said. 'That was his name. I'm Mrs Phillips, you see.'

'And what sort of thing did he—just a minute! Did you say your name was Phillips?'

'Yes, that's right.'

'Are you telling me that your husband who wrote books about the Bible was J.B. Phillips?'

'Yes, that's right. J.B. Phillips. He did quite a lot of translations of the Bible.'

He certainly did. J.B. Phillips had been one of my early heroes. *Letters to Young Churches* was his version of the New Testament epistles. Then there were *The Gospels in Modern English* and *The Young Church in Action*, the latter being a translation of the book of Acts. Phillips had brought the New Testament alive with a style and vividness that captured the attention and the hearts of a whole generation of Christians. C.S. Lewis, scholar, author and Christian apologist, had much admired Phillips' work. He commented in a letter to the translator that reading the new versions was like seeing a painting, a familiar old master, after it has been cleaned, and appreciating its colours and content properly for the first time.

As I looked down into the smiling face of the elderly lady in front of me, I was conscious of having one question that I was burning to ask—and this might be the only chance I would ever get. My question was about Phillips and Lewis. As far as I could remember, Lewis and Phillips had corresponded but never actually met, but there was an extraordinary account by Phillips of meeting or being confronted by Lewis *after* the great man's death. The translator had been sitting in his study, puzzling over some aspect of his work, when Lewis appeared, sitting in the chair opposite, pipe in hand, looking content and ruddier than ever and offering Phillips advice to the effect that it (the translation problem? Christian belief? life itself?) was much simpler than he thought.

Evangelical Christians are a funny breed. We rant and rave about what invariably happens, and what never happens, and what ought always to happen, and what the Bible definitely says and what it definitely doesn't say, and then, right in the middle of all this certainty (because, like everyone else, we have rich hearts and imaginations as well as our silly little heads), we go and make exceptions! This business of Phillips and Lewis is a good example. I can recall conversations with believers who would categorically rule out all possibility of contact with the dead, but were somehow easily able to accommodate the encounter I have just described. The popularity of Lionel Blue with fairly fundamentalist believers is another example. They might normally have a great deal to say about gay issues and the errancy of Jewish belief, but this gay rabbi has distracted and disarmed them with his wisdom and his compassionate heart. He has become a sort of honorary Christian. It does us all a tremendous amount of good to be disarmed at times—just for a little while.

Anyway, back to my question.

'Your husband gave a wonderful gift to the church,' I said. Then I paused, worried that I was being a little presumptuous. 'Look, we may never meet again, so—I hope you don't mind, could I just ask you a question?'

'Yes, of course you can. What would you like to know?'

'Well, your husband recorded how C.S. Lewis appeared to him in his study once, didn't he?'

She nodded. 'That's right.'

'My question is—do you think that really happened? In your opinion, did that meeting take place?'

'I was there in the room at the time,' said Mrs Phillips simply.

'So did you see Lewis as well?'

'I didn't actually see him,' she replied, 'but I heard all of my husband's side of the conversation, and afterwards he told me who he had been talking to.'

'Thank you,' I said as I shook her hand once more. 'Thank you very much.'

Did J.B. Phillips see C.S. Lewis sitting in his study in the early 1960s? If so, did he imagine it, or was it really Lewis, popping in to offer a helping hand to his fellow writer? No one can say for sure— not me, not Mrs Phillips, not anyone—but isn't it fascinating? And if we are to believe that all these holy men came out of their graves and were seen and recognized by lots of people in the city, what is the difference? Lewis was a sort of holy man.

I loathe all aspects of spiritualism, and I have never in my life, certainly not in my waking hours, ever seen anyone who used to be dead, but miracles did not come to an end when the ink of the last full stop of the last sentence of scripture was finally dry, so who knows? By his death and resurrection, Jesus created a great and glorious connection between life on both sides of the grave. Decisions about how that connection might be used are, as always, in the hands of God.

Don't forget

Jesus overcame death. If the curtain were to be drawn back, we might be amazed at how insubstantial many of our concerns about life and death really are. Heaven is a short bridge away, and he will be there to lead us across.

THROUGH THE DARK GLASS

When Israel was a child, I loved him,
and out of Egypt I called my son.
But the more they were called,
the more they went away from me.
They sacrificed to the Baals
and they burned incense to images.
It was I who taught Ephraim to walk,
taking them by the arms;
but they did not realize
it was I who healed them.
I led them with cords of human kindness,
with ties of love. To them I was like one who lifts
a little child to the cheek,
and I bent down to feed them.

HOSEA 11:1–4 (TNIV)

I will have no compassion,
even though he thrives among his brothers.
An east wind from the Lord will come,
blowing in from the desert;
his spring will fail
and his well dry up.
His storehouse will be plundered
of all its treasures.
The people of Samaria must bear their guilt,
because they have rebelled against their God.
They will fall by the sword;
their little ones will be dashed to the ground,
their pregnant women ripped open.

HOSEA 13:14b–16

I will heal their waywardness
and love them freely,
for my anger has turned away from them.
I will be like the dew to Israel;
he will blossom like a lily.
Like a cedar of Lebanon
he will send down his roots;
his young shoots will grow.
His splendour will be like an olive tree,
his fragrance like a cedar of Lebanon.
People will dwell again in his shade;
they will flourish like the corn,
they will blossom like the vine—
Israel's fame will be like the wine of Lebanon.
Ephraim, what more have I to do with idols?
I will answer him and care for him.
I am like a flourishing juniper;
your fruitfulness comes from me.

HOSEA 14:4–8 (TNIV)

It was the second passage in this trio from Hosea that originally caught my eye. It really has been most interesting to stroll through the Bible, consciously making the effort not to do a little hop of avoidance when I come to obstacles that would otherwise trip me up. This is one of those obstacles, and its existence has been lodged uncomfortably in the back of my mind for years. These verses tell us that because of God's anger little children will be dashed to the ground, and pregnant women will be ripped open.

It's horrible. Grotesque. It makes me feel sick. How could the God that I think I know lend his name to such unspeakable things? Has he lent his name to them? Should we assume that because these words are in the Bible, we must accept them? What does acceptance actually mean? Lots of questions. Where can we go hunting for answers?

Before I started writing this morning, I had a phone call from a friend who lives in America. I'll call him Jack. Jack is a formidably clever, good-looking young man who should have achieved great things by now, both academically and in whatever line of work he might have chosen to pursue. Jack is a Christian, but he had a desperately troubled childhood, and the worst aspects of these troubles have continued to haunt him through the years. Additionally, over the last decade he has suffered from a severe mental illness, the main sympton being a morbid obsession with the ultimate fate of his own body. What will happen to it after he dies? Will God look after that sad little body that was so badly abused all those years ago? Will Jesus really be there to make sure Jack is all right?

As a result of carefully adjusted medication, Jack has had one or two longish periods of relief from his illness, but every now and then everything falls apart again, and that is what has happened just recently. When he is in this state, almost anything can trigger an obsessional phase of behaviour. At these points he will sometimes phone me. This morning it was one of the Psalms. Jack had happened to read the 88th Psalm, probably the most unremittingly dark and despairing piece in the whole canon. It includes these words (vv. 3–5):

> *I am overwhelmed with troubles*
> *and my life draws near to death.*
> *I am counted among those who go down to the pit;*
> *I am like one without strength.*
> *I am set apart with the dead,*
> *like the slain who lie in the grave,*
> *whom you remember no more,*
> *who are cut off from your care.*

Obsessional behaviour is very similar to jealous behaviour in that people thus afflicted will hunt feverishly and indefatigably for evidence to support the conclusion that they most dread. Jack had probably hunted fearfully through the Bible like a child lost in a cave, searching for such evidence. Now, unfortunately, he had found it. The very thought of being left in a grave, separated from God and cut off for ever from his care, was just about as bad as it could get.

'The thing is,' said Jack, his voice tense with that odd mix of apology and frantic appeal that I had become so used to, 'some people will tell you that the Bible is—you know—completely inspired by God. Every word is meant, and it's all him speaking. And if that really is true, then surely God is speaking to me through the words in this psalm, isn't he?'

One of the good things about Jack is that he has a huge regard for Jesus. Another is that, because he really is very clever, it is always possible to appeal to his sense of logic. Logic will not heal Jack, but it will give him a means by which he can temporarily survive. What could I say? How could I appeal to those two things I knew about him?

'Jack,' I said, 'you really love Jesus, don't you?'

'Yes,' he replied, 'I do.'

'Well, he is the nearest and clearest picture of God that we've got. So when you're reading the Bible you should always start with him, and then work backwards or forwards. Read all those wonderful reassuring things he says to his disciples at the end of John's Gospel before you go anywhere near any other part of the Bible. Will you promise to try to do that?'

'Yes,' said Jack, 'I will try, but this psalm—'

'Jack, tell me something. When you read what someone like King Herod says in the Gospels, do you think that's God talking? Is that God speaking through him?'

'No, it's not. It's Herod.'

'So why is it in the Bible?'

'I suppose because God wanted it to be there.'

'Exactly. God isn't cruel and nasty like Herod, but he wants us to know what Herod said, because it's all part of the story. And the psalms are the same. They're poems and songs written by people who were going through all sorts of different experiences. The man who wrote the psalm you've been worrying about was a man with a huge problem, but it was *his* problem, and he was using those words to tell God about his deepest, darkest fears. God wants them there in the Bible because we can learn a lot about ourselves and about him by reading what others have written. Some of the psalms are tragic, but most of them end with a burst of optimism, don't they?'

'Yes, I suppose they do...'

I don't know if any of this helped Jack, but it certainly helped me. These three passages from Hosea, embodying sadness, wild fury and deep compassion, are extravagant and passionate in their content and style, and I have no doubt that they seek to reflect genuine aspects of God. At the same time, I believe it is necessary to bear in mind that they were actually written by a man—Hosea himself, perhaps—and that the glass he saw through was as dark as the one that Paul mentions in 1 Corinthians 13 (the King James version). I thank God for the book of Hosea, and I am sure it is there for a purpose, but if you wish to tell me that the God I meet in Jesus gets so wildly angry that he rips open pregnant women, then I shall not agree with you.

A prayer

Father, I am very good at getting things wrong, but until you tell me face to face that I am wrong in this matter I cannot depart from the view that is expressed here. As a father, of course you will be angry with your children from time to time, but we know that your anger has its roots in love, and we thank you for the passion and compassion with which you regard us. Help us to be grateful and obedient so that, instead of deserving your anger, we can live in peace with you.

LESSONS FOR
THE CHURCH

---------------- ✤ ----------------

LIARS!

If we claim to be without sin, we deceive ourselves and the truth is not in us. If we confess our sins, he is faithful and just and will forgive us our sins and purify us from all unrighteousness. If we claim we have not sinned, we make him out to be a liar and his word has no place in our lives.

My dear children, I write this to you so that you will not sin. But if anybody does sin, we have one who speaks to the Father in our defence—Jesus Christ, the Righteous One.

1 JOHN 1:8—2:1

Can we really believe these familiar words? I have already said a lot about telling the truth in a previous chapter, but here is another little story on that subject that may help us to answer my question.

There were seven for lunch—myself, my wife, my 17-year-old daughter and a friend with her three children, aged from ten to five. Eventually, for no very good reason that I can remember, I asked a question: 'How many of us tell lies?'

Seven hands went up! No hesitation. All of us, from the oldest (me) to the youngest, aged five, instantly acknowledged our occasional excursions from the truth. The children, charming and well brought up, were bonelessly casual about it. Of course they told lies. One even laughed, as though the idea of surviving this wild world on a meagre diet of truth was silly—ridiculous. It was rather striking and, accordingly, I was rather struck.

Of course, I reflected, some might see cause for alarm in this lunchtime revelation. Seven Christian people, adults and children, had confessed to the presence of some virulent dishonesty virus. Perhaps, but I found myself asking a question. Why were we seven liars being so very open and honest about our capacity for telling lies? The paradox amused and bemused me. I thought about this for the whole of the rest of that day, and eventually I realized that there was probably one overwhelming reason for such willing veracity. We were comfortable. All of us felt comfortable enough in that situation and with those people to tell the truth without fear of being condemned or pushed crudely into the swamp of guilt that is always so destructive to the peace of Christians.

Simultaneously with this thought, my eyes were reopened to an old truth. I began my Christian life by accepting my identity as a sinner, and I know that it would be foolish to assume that the same pattern will not be repeated again and again for the rest of my life. John says in this passage that if we claim to be without sin we deceive ourselves, but that when we do acknowledge our sin, Jesus will deal with it. Many of us, however, have a great deal of difficulty in accepting that this really is so. How can God go on and on and on forgiving us every day, often when we have committed the same old sins for the 490th time? The answer is that he can because he wants to.

The lesson we might learn from that lunch for liars is that we never can be settled with God until we become truly comfortable with the relationship that he has decided on and which he freely offers to us. And no, of course I don't mean that we can take a relaxed attitude to sin. But I do mean that we can take a relaxed attitude to forgiveness. God has adopted us. We are his children. He readily accepts the challenge of dealing with us. We accept his claim on us. We sit around his table, as the seven of us sat around the table the other day, and we raise our hands readily when called to confession.

'That's fine,' says God. 'Well done. Now we can start again.'

If, occasionally, we laugh at some point in this process, he will understand that we do it because we sense, more perhaps than at any other time, how much we are loved.

A prayer

Thank you so much, Father, that you have made it possible for us to sit comfortably with you and be honest about our failures and weaknesses. We know that you hate sin, but we also know that you sent Jesus for the express purpose of mending the relationship between earth and heaven. We will let you be a Father to us, and be glad that we really can be adopted members of your family. Please help those who are trapped in their sin and cannot believe that forgiveness is so close at hand.

———————— ✦ ————————

MADE FOR US

God saw all that he had made, and it was very good. And there was evening, and there was morning—the sixth day.

Thus the heavens and the earth were completed in all their vast array.

By the seventh day God had finished the work he had been doing; so on that seventh day he rested from all his work. And God blessed the seventh day and made it holy, because on it he rested from all the work of creating that he had done.

GENESIS 1:31—2:3

A rant.

There is a natural tendency to accept automatically the teaching given by those who were instrumental in your conversion. This can be useful. Many lessons I learned as a teenager are solid stone blocks in the foundation of my faith. I am grateful for them. The other side of this particular coin, though, is the difficulty of adapting ideas that were concreted in, all those years ago. When concrete gets old, it tends to become cracked, uneven and ugly. It needs to be removed, and sometimes we discover to our amazement and delight that the original surface is far more attractive than its artificial covering.

This is very commonly true with the unhealthy tension experienced by many of us over the business of minding our Christian

'P's and 'Q's. Well meaning though leaders and teachers may be, there is always a danger of defaulting to wariness and warnings about the undesirability of being naughty and making God cross. This juvenile model can last a lifetime. I have met so many people who need to be set free from the idea that they have only been accepted into the kingdom by the skin of their teeth, and could easily be slung out if they fail to dot all the 'i's and cross all the 't's in their rather rigidly contained walk with Christ. Being a father myself, I have seen and understood the necessity to juggle discipline and freedom so that my children behave well but are not nervously weighed down by slabs of concrete that shut off their spontaneity and creative impulses. I am quite sure that I have not been totally successful in doing this, but I have tried. And as for slinging them out—let's not be silly.

For Christians, it can be almost miraculously refreshing to discover that the weight they have been carrying never was necessary, and that the person underneath is actually more attractive to God and everyone else than they could ever have believed.

Yes, some things need re-examining, and this passage embodies one of them. For years, I barely glanced at these verses. I knew what I had been told. Sunday was for serious engagement with God and quiet relaxation. Recreation, sports and trips to the cinema or the pub were unsuitable for the Lord's Day. There came a time, however, when I realized that, inwardly, I had actually not agreed with this view for years.

I am a writer, so I rest from creating on Sunday as well. My work may not be quite on a par with creating the universe, I grudgingly grant you, but there are similarities. Surely, on that seventh day, God enjoyed and relished the good things he had made. At the weekend I need to do things that make me come alive again. I certainly do not need to shut myself down and try to worship God out of my misery. The sabbath was made for humans, said Jesus, not humans for the sabbath. It is for us. Got it? Resting from the things that we normally do doesn't mean that we do nothing. It means that we reinvigorate our souls and bodies and minds with activities (church attendance included) that make us more human rather than less. It is a rich blessing from God and we should jolly well enjoy it. I bet he did and does. There is nothing holy about tedium.

End of rant.

A prayer

Father, thank you for establishing a day of rest. Whichever part of the week we are obliged to take it on, we praise you for the richness of love and life. May our sabbath time be a period of genuine relaxation and recreation, as you always intended it to be. We pray for those who are still struggling under all sorts of unnecessary burdens, that they will find release and freedom to enjoy their lives with you. Thank you, Father.

---- ❖ ----

WHOSE FAITH?

Jesus left there and went to his home town, accompanied by his disciples. When the Sabbath came, he began to teach in the synagogue, and many who heard him were amazed.

'Where did this man get these things?' they asked. 'What's this wisdom that has been given him? What are these remarkable miracles he is performing? Isn't this the carpenter? Isn't this Mary's son and the brother of James, Joseph, Judas and Simon? Aren't his sisters here with us?' And they took offence at him.

Jesus said to them, 'Only in their own towns, among their relatives and in their own homes are prophets without honour.' He could not do any miracles there, except lay his hands on a few people who were ill and heal them. He was amazed at their lack of faith.

MARK 6:1–6a (TNIV)

I remember noticing this passage when I first became interested in following Jesus, at the age of 16. It didn't seem to make very much sense to me then, but I assumed that older, wiser Christians must understand it, and that I would share their insights in the fullness of time. In fact, this tended to be my response to just about every inexplicable aspect of the faith that I had begun to embrace, and there were certainly some areas where that optimism was justified. Many of the knots did unravel themselves as time went by, and very satisfying that process has proved to be. I love untangling knots, especially when it becomes excitingly possible to fly your kite as a result. Some of these tangled issues hung around, however, and a few remain to the present day, largely because I have a bad habit of letting my mind just slide away from such problems whenever I encounter them. This passage embodies one of those knotty questions.

I honestly cannot understand what is going on here, but I am determined to try. Why was Jesus unable to perform many miracles because the people of Nazareth lacked faith? To be honest, at first sight it tends to give a rather thin feel to the whole of his ministry. Did his miracles really depend on a certain level of faith in those for whom he prayed? Why on earth should a lacklustre response dampen the capacity of the Son of God for bringing supernatual assistance to those who needed it?

It is undoubtedly true that Jesus frequently commended people for their depth of belief, and he definitely attributed healing and forgiveness to their level of faith, or, as in the case of the man lowered through the roof, the faith of their friends or family. Nevertheless, as I do a quick mental scan of the Gospel stories, I recall a number of other occasions when the miracles that Jesus performed seemed to have little or nothing to do with the faith of the recipient. Bringing the son of the widow of Nain back to life is one example. I have just looked it up. This is how Luke records the incident (7:12–15, TNIV).

As he approached the town gate, a dead person was being carried out—the only son of his mother, and she was a widow. And a large crowd from the town was with her. When the Lord saw her, his heart went out to her and he said, 'Don't cry.'

Then he went up and touched the bier they were carrying him on, and the bearers stood still. He said, 'Young man, I say to you, get up!' The dead man sat up and began to talk, and Jesus gave him back to his mother.

A lovely little story—one of my favourites. Once again I smile as I read that the dead man sat up and began to talk. 'Now, where was I before I was so rudely interrupted?' might well have been his first words. What I love most about this story, though, is the compassionate immediacy of Jesus' response to the weeping mother. His heart went out to her. 'Don't cry,' he said, and within seconds the boy was restored to life. So warm, so human, so helpful.

Well, going back to the subject of our discussion, the boy can't have been displaying much faith, can he? He was dead, poor chap. And the mother was all wrapped up in her grief: not much belief emanating from that quarter. Who had the faith for this miracle? Jesus did. He wanted to heal the boy, and so he did. Other examples include the servant who lost his ear in the garden when Jesus was arrested, and the five thousand who needed feeding on the hillside. I very much doubt that anyone but Jesus himself had the faith to believe in this latter extraordinary miracle. Not even Jamie Oliver would have been optimistic enough to undertake such a catering extravaganza using such meagre resources. It might also be worth recording that John Wimber was practically drained of faith on the first occasion when someone actually recovered as a response to one of his prayers.

So there it is. Having faith does seem to be extremely helpful when you need a miracle, but not always. Surely Jesus has the power of the Creator at his disposal. He can do what he likes. Why, then, did he have so much trouble with the locals when he visited his home town? According to this passage, he was unable to perform many miracles. It was not a matter of choice: he simply was *not able* to do it. Furthermore, he was amazed at their lack of faith. Amazed. Surprised. Shocked. Omnipotence and omniscience are bedrocks in the nature of God, but these attributes were clearly not present or active in Jesus at this juncture. What can we say? As I sit and think about all this, a couple of things spring to mind.

First, like many others, I have an unfortunate knee-jerk reaction to the proposition that people need faith in order to be supernaturally healed. For years, many of us have battled against the idea that sick or disabled folk who 'disappoint' would-be agents of healing can be dismissed as failures on the basis that they must be lacking faith if they have not been healed. And, broadly speaking, we have been right to battle against this notion. Those who sustain it are all too often motivated by a thinly disguised hunger for power and success. They are not interested in people. They are interested in being significant and powerful and in being right and in being seen to be right. Over the years, they have badly hurt many, many suffering folk who trusted them in vain. I have met many of these victims.

I guess the problem is that, as usual, we have tended to discard an important point for fear of over-emphasizing it. Faith is a key element in the healing of individuals in the New Testament, despite the kinds of exception we have already looked at. Anything that builds up our faith will make us more accessible to miraculous works of God in our lives. Perhaps we need to be more accepting of that fact, as well as happily acknowledging and rejoicing in the fact that there are times when God decides to *do it*, regardless of who has faith and who has not.

That's one point. Another is that, once again, we are reminded in this passage of the impenetrably mysterious fact that Jesus was truly man as well as being truly God. I don't know about you, but over and over again I land on this tension, this teasing conundrum, this glorious impossibility. How can it be that a concept so strange and so difficult to grasp is able to provide me with solid ground at those times when everything else is shimmering and shifting and becoming insubstantial? I have no real answer to that question, except that it locks into my spirit like a dovetail joint, or like the last spanner in the box that really does fit the immovable nut. The genuine humanity of Jesus has infuriated and reassured men and women for centuries. It draws and repels now as it did when he walked the earth.

No corners were cut in the great salvation plan. God did actually, in great humility, and for reasons of love, become a real man with real limits and a real capacity for being amazed. Let us not bother trying to understand the ultimate meaning of that fact. We won't be able to. We can, however, savour and appreciate the mysterious rightness of it. So odd, and so wonderful.

A prayer

Thank you, Father, for showing me how the very area that has seemed troublesome illustrates one of the central aspects of spiritual stability and safety. Because you loved us, you really did roll your sleeves up and become an authentic human being. What an adventure! What an experience! Teach us how to live, bemused but confident, in the centre of the paradox.

---------- ✢ ----------

MORE THAN ONE KIND OF PRAYER

'You have spoken arrogantly against me,' says the Lord.

'Yet you ask, "What have we said against you?"

You have said, "It is futile to serve God. What do we gain by carrying out his requirements and going about like mourners before the Lord Almighty? But now we call the arrogant blessed. Certainly evildoers prosper, and even when they put God to the test, they get away with it."'

Then those who feared the Lord talked with each other, and the Lord listened and heard. A scroll of remembrance was written in his presence concerning those who feared the Lord and honoured his name.

'On the day when I act,' says the Lord Almighty, 'they will be my treasured possession. I will spare them, just as a father has compassion and spares his son who serves him. And you will again see the distinction between the righteous and the wicked, between those who serve God and those who do not.'

MALACHI 3:13–18 (TNIV)

Theoretically, we improve as we get older. The theory holds good for me in certain areas. For instance, I have finally leaned how to make the cardboard flap on one side of the top of a cereal packet fit into the little slot on the other side. I am proud of this. In other areas, I do not improve. I deteriorate. Take prayer. Private prayer is fine. I'm always nattering on to God. Nor do I mind formal, liturgical prayer. Much of it is elegant and meaningful, and I love it. Praying from the front of my own church is one of my favourite things, and I also quite enjoy times of open prayer during services. All those things are fine. No, my problem is with extemporary prayer in small groups.

I realized how bad it was getting the other day when I had to travel several miles from home to discuss a forthcoming festival with members of the church where the event was being held. It was a very good meeting—warm, busy and useful. The other five people involved were bright, practical and friendly. The coffee was strong and flavoursome, just as I adore it, and the lunch was greater in quality and quantity than it needed to be, exactly as all good lunches should be. After our meal, another hour of discussion was scheduled, followed by a period of prayer before we went our separate ways. It was during that final hour of discussion that I began to feel a little uncomfortable. Pretty soon, the vicar who was chairing the meeting so charmingly would be asking us to bow our heads and talk to God about the things that had been brought up during the day. It was a good idea, of course—how could it not be? Everything we wanted to accomplish was for him. So why was I feeling so twitchy about the prospect?

It's hard to answer that question. When it comes to honesty in these areas, there are layers below layers below layers. What I do know is that nowadays in these situations my brain seems to get scrambled and my tongue responds accordingly by tying itself in knots. It's horrible. And, though I say it myself, I used to be very good at this sort of prayer. Mind you, that was during a part of my life when I was mainly concerned about the opinions of others. You should have heard the prayers I uttered in small groups in those days, you really should. They were fantastic. Some of them were so dramatic, and so passionate, and so fluent, and so bogus. Maybe, I reflected, as the vicar issued the invitation for us to pray, after years spent consciously performing in these situations, I have come to doubt the integrity of my own utterances. I truly do not believe it is just that, though.

There is also a growing awareness in me that prayer is, or can be, a much broader and richer experience than I had realized. And it is confirmed by words from this passage that I have never properly registered until now. These people who feared the Lord and knew that their attitudes had been wrong came together and talked to each other about what they might do to put things right. The Lord, we are told, listened and heard. The implicit suggestion, a refreshing one for me, is that when conversation is honestly and devoutly dedicated to God, it is heard by him as though it was prayer. They talked together and God, having listened to what they said, got a secretarial angel to take down their names.

Paradoxically, this realization by no means inclines me to believe that we have no need for the kind of extemporary prayer that I am so bad at nowadays. On the contrary, I feel much more relaxed with the notion that direct prayer at the end of a discussion is merely a continuation of the process by which we offer ourselves and every word that we say to God.

A thought

Obviously all kinds of prayer can be good and useful, but perhaps every word that we say and every action that we perform should be an expression of ourselves to God. It's not easy, because we are pretty sure that he doesn't want some of the grottier words and deeds, but I suspect that he would prefer us to leave the editing process to him.

---------------- ✛ ----------------

KNOWING ME, KNOWING YOU

'Not everyone who says to me, "Lord, Lord," will enter the kingdom of heaven, but only those who do the will of my Father who is in heaven. Many will say to me on that day, "Lord, Lord, did we not prophesy in your name and in your name drive out demons and in your name perform many miracles?" Then I will tell them plainly, "I never knew you. Away from me, you evildoers!"'

MATTHEW 7:21–23

During a trip that Bridget and I made to Bangladesh a few years ago, we saw some remarkable sights. Chief among these was the work being done to rescue homeless little girls from the filthy streets that criss-cross the slums of Dhaka. Many of these children have never known a kind word in the past, and inevitably there will be some, a few very young indeed, who will drift into prostitution in order to keep their bodies alive. The project that we found was run by two women, one a Christian and the other a Muslim. I have frequently made the point that neither of these women will ever write paperbacks for the religious market, nor will they deliver seminars in large leaky tents at spiritual conferences. They are simply there, grappling with a never-ending, enormously taxing task, using the bare minimum of resources needed for the job. They are wonderful people and I am in awe of them. I suspect that they are too busy to give much attention to their religious differences—which brings us to an inevitable question. Are they both going to heaven?

Orthodox evangelical Christianity is quite clear on this point, and let me assure you in all seriousness that nobody I know is a jot more orthodox than I am. As the years pass, I become increasingly convinced that there is one way and one way only into the presence of God. Jesus is the way, the truth and the life. His death paid for our sins, and we shall be resurrected just as he was, if his life lives in us and we are obedient to him. No man or woman comes to the Father except through Jesus, and that is that. End of argument. That is what I believe.

Here is something else that I believe. I believe that the Muslim woman who rescues and cares for little girls in the slums of Dhaka will be in heaven one day. Let me explain my reasons for saying this.

C.S. Lewis famously stated that there will be some surprises in heaven, and I have to agree with him. Some of these surprises will undoubtedly be focused on who *is* there, but perhaps the greatest shocks of all will concern those who are not. The people mentioned in this passage from Matthew are a very good example. These will be folk who probably said all the right prayers, including one in which they invited Jesus into their lives. They sang all the right choruses, took all the right public attitudes, exercised dramatic ministries in healing and deliverance and acquired great fame as representatives and preachers of the gospel of Jesus Christ. But it will be revealed that the things they did and the words they said actually flowed from a source that had nothing to do with the Spirit of Jesus, and their ultimate effect on vulnerable souls will be one of potential darkness and destruction. Let us beware—all those of us who are privileged to have opportunities to write about, or preach, or teach, or sing, or in any other way communicate the Christian faith. Many of us have stepped into the trap of substituting a personal agenda for the initiatives of God. This internal conjuring trick may bring rewards of power, fame, personal achievement and perhaps even wealth in this lifetime, but I don't ever want to hear Jesus say that he never knew me. Do you? Of course not.

That brings me directly to the blind spot in this passage and my confidence in the heavenly destination of that Muslim woman. Consider the implication of those four frightening words that Jesus speaks in this passage.

'I never knew you.'

It has only just occurred to me that he did not say, 'I never knew you, and you never knew me.' We must always be careful about drawing massive inferences from fragments of scripture, but Jesus does appear to be suggesting here that when we finally encounter him, the question of whether *he knows us* will be the centrally important issue. In case this is all beginning to sound rather compli-cated, just have a look at these verses from a later chapter of the same Gospel.

'Then the King will say to those on his right, "Come, you who are blessed by my Father; take your inheritance, the kingdom prepared for you since the creation of the world. For I was hungry and you gave me something to eat, I was thirsty and you gave me something to drink, I was a stranger and you invited me in, I needed clothes and you clothed me, I was ill and you looked after me, I was in prison and you came to visit me."

'Then the righteous will answer him, "Lord, when did we see you hungry and feed you, or thirsty and give you something to drink? When did we see you a stranger and invite you in, or needing clothes and clothe you? When did we see you ill or in prison and go to visit you?"

'The King will reply, "Truly I tell you, whatever you did for one of the least of these brothers and sisters of mine, you did for me."'
MATTHEW 25:34–40 (TNIV)

What will Jesus say to that anonymous Muslim woman when he meets her at the gates of heaven? Something like this, perhaps?

'I know you. When nobody else cared, you picked me up from those horrible streets in the slum and you took me to a place that was light and bright and fresh. It was so wonderful and so unexpected. You gave me clean clothes to wear and food to eat. You taught me to play games and musical instruments. You spoke to me as if I was not just a scrap of rubbish to be used and then thrown aside. You looked at me with warmth in your eyes and made me feel that one day I really might be valuable to someone.'

And she will feel bewildered and say to him, 'Lord, I don't understand. When did I pick you up from the streets, and do all these other things?'

He will reply, 'Every time you did it for the smallest and most helpless of these little sisters of mine, you did it for me.'

Then, perhaps, she will look more closely at his face and exclaim, 'Oh, it's you! Now I remember…'

Let me repeat what I have already said. Jesus is the only way. That is what I believe. We need to preach that fact of faith wherever we go, and be aware that souls will be saved when men and women reach out to him in faith and obedience. But let us also be aware that he is the Lord. He is in charge. He is the one who truly knows the hearts of every one of us. I may think I hold every spiritual qualification under the sun for my claim that I know him and that I am heading for heaven, but in the end, only one thing will matter. Does he know me?

A prayer

Father, we thank you for all those folk who give their time and resources so generously to people who have been rejected by the rest of the world. Forgive us for making cheap judgments about your attitude to them when we are doing so much less to relieve the burdens of those who are crushed by poverty and disease. Thank you that Jesus is the only way by which any human being can come home to you. We pray from the bottom of our hearts that your agenda will be ours, and that our obedience and faithfulness will be rewarded on that good day when the Lord Jesus greets us personally and says, 'I know you.'

❖

DEAD OR ALIVE

To the angel of the church in Sardis write:

These are the words of him who holds the seven spirits of God and the seven stars. I know your deeds; you have a reputation of being alive, but you are dead. Wake up! Strengthen what remains and is about to die, for

I have not found your deeds complete in the sight of my God. Remember, therefore, what you have received and heard; obey it, and repent. But if you do not wake up, I will come like a thief, and you will not know at what time I will come to you.

REVELATION 3:1–3

I don't know about you, but if I'm not careful I can waste hours and hours over verses like this. I can remember it happening to me with a number of passages. That bit in the seventh chapter of Matthew about sheep in wolves' clothing, for instance. When I was a young Christian, I got myself into a real state about the possibility that I might be secretly motivated by evil in my dealings with other Christians. I probably used up a lot of valuable time worrying about this, time that could have been more usefully employed in doing things I had postponed in the first place. Thank God, common sense prevailed in the end, but it wasn't long before I transferred my nervous attention to Luke 9, where Jesus says that no one who puts his hand to the plough and then looks back is fit for service in the kingdom of God.

'Does that apply to looking back just once,' I asked my troubled self, 'or would you get a few warnings before being fired—if that's the word? And now I think about it, I'm pretty sure I've already looked back lots of times, so the chances are I've already been excluded from the kingdom of God.'

Wise counsel dragged me out of that particular pit. I think it was something along the lines of, 'Shut up and get on with it.'

So how about this passage from Revelation in particular? Tough stuff, eh? To be honest, I've never really enjoyed reading the lamp-stand/candlestick section of the last book of the Bible. It's too much like a game of Cluedo that ends up with me having done it all, everywhere. And it's yet another example of those extracts from scripture that so effortlessly induce guilt in people like myself and send us into a troubled spin. I usually start a fierce inward debate.

'Do you have a reputation for being alive?'

'Well, I've written this book and lots of others about Jesus, haven't I? Isn't that a public claim, even a boast, to be spiritually alive in some way?'

'Yes, but you do go out of your way to be endearingly self-effacing from time to time.'

'You make it sound so calculating. Anyway, that's not the same as being dead, is it?'

'Of course not. So, are you dead?'

'I don't think so.'

'I see, and you say that because…?'

'Because I really care about whether I am or I'm not.'

And that's where my particular debate on this subject invariably ends. Nowadays it matters to me that God cares about what I do and think and feel. Increasingly, I am far less concerned with what anyone else thinks. As I have said, it concerns me that many of us use up valuable time on these knee-jerk reactions to verses that were never meant to trigger guilt in the wrong people. Do you want to be truly alive? I bet you do. Do you want to be secretly dead? I bet you don't. We have quite enough to repent of without getting lost in this sort of thing.

A prayer

Lord, let me be always ready to face the things that are genuinely wrong with me, and give me the discernment to avoid wasting time with the things that are not.

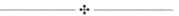

USELESS FIRES

'Now implore God to be gracious to us. With such offerings from your hands, will he accept you?'—says the Lord Almighty.

'Oh, that one of you would shut the temple doors, so that you would not light useless fires on my altar! I am not pleased with you,' says the Lord Almighty, 'and I will accept no offering from your hands. My name will be great among the nations, from where the sun rises to where it sets. In every place incense and pure offerings will be brought to me, because my name will be great among the nations,' says the Lord Almighty.

'But you profane it by saying, 'The Lord's table is defiled,' and, 'Its food is contemptible.' And you say, 'What a burden!' and you sniff at it contemptuously,' says the Lord Almighty.

MALACHI 1:9–13A (TNIV)

'Useless fires.' The phrase jumped out at me. How many useless fires are lit in Christian churches around the world every Sunday, fires that crackle and pop and are filled with colour, but offer no genuine heat to the chilled body of Christ? This can happen for many reasons. I remember, for instance, speaking at a church on the borders of Scotland and England where the worship time preceding my talk was about as perfect in technical musical terms as it could be. The music rose and fell and ebbed and flowed with flawless precision, while the singers sang so skilfully and in such perfect harmony that it was a joy to listen. And yet...

What is the element missing from otherwise excellent church music when it just does not work? That was my feeling as I sat and listened to the instrumentalists and the vocalists. Something essential was absent from all those carefully organized sounds. Spiritual confidence, perhaps? A detachment from the roots of worship? A lack of heart? I found out later. Days earlier, the minister of the church had admitted to long-term adultery with a member of his congregation, and the technical near-perfection of the music was a desperate attempt to paper over deep cracks that had opened in the church community. That worship session never reached heaven and it never left the ground. Facts and feelings need to be faced. Tears and silence would have been more useful. It was a useless fire, and it warmed nobody.

A very similar point is made in the first chapter of Isaiah.

'The multitude of your sacrifices—what are they to me?' says the Lord. 'I have more than enough of burnt offerings, of rams and the fat of fattened animals; I have no pleasure in the blood of bulls and lambs and goats…

'I will not listen. Your hands are full of blood; wash and make yourselves clean. Take your evil deeds out of my sight! Stop doing wrong, learn to do right! Seek justice, encourage the oppressed. Defend the cause of the fatherless, plead the case of the widow.'

ISAIAH 1:11, 15B–17

'Look,' says God, 'I don't actually want any of that stuff. I really don't. It does nothing for me. What I want is for you to be just and kind and to look after the poor. I would like you to be obedient. My Son was obedient to the point of death and that's why I'm able to welcome you home. Don't waste what he did. I wouldn't give you two pence for religion, not even some of the wild, sizzling stuff that's taken the place of burning animals nowadays. Be loving to me and to each other. That's the scent I love—and have always loved.'

This is a voice that many Christians do not want to hear. It's too natural, too godly, too liable to insinuate itself into the cracks between our humanity and our faith, supergluing the two together, making us whole but robbing us of all the old securities.

Scary and sweet, isn't it? Clearly, God has never been interested in useless fire, flowery words, hollow worship or religious camouflage. He wants us to get on with the things that really matter. It might also be worth reflecting on this well-known verse from James: 'Religion that God our Father accepts as pure and faultless is this: to look after orphans and widows in their distress and to keep oneself from being polluted by the world' (1:27).

When my wife and I travelled to Zambia in 2004, the significance of this verse became all too apparent. The purpose of our trip was to look at the work being done by World Vision, particularly in connection with the AIDS pandemic that is devastating the population in that part of the world. The idea was to write a book about our experiences that would highlight the enormous need for more resources, not just in Africa but in many other parts of the world as well.

We saw sights and people that came close to breaking our hearts. As one local worker told us, the fabric of Africa is being torn apart. Because of poverty and sickness, it is often the case that children are no longer being taken in and cared for by relatives. On the contrary, there are many instances of houses and property being taken away from orphans, who are then left to fend for themselves in a world where there are no hand-outs, unless you are fortunate enough to benefit from what is being done by the many aid agencies that are undertaking inspiring but inadequate work in that part of the world. Widows are dying of AIDS and wondering what will happen to their children when they have gone. We met some of them. Young children are caring for their younger brothers and sisters because there is no one else left to do it. Like many countries that lie under the dark shadow of the AIDS crisis, Zambia is full of widows and orphans in distress. Food, health facilities, self-sustaining projects and education are priorities in these places, but there is not enough money.

Do I believe what James says about true religion? Yes, I do. Am I aware of the crisis in countries like Zambia? Yes, I am. What will I do? I shall stop studying my spiritual navel and sponsor a child. It costs less than £20 each month. If we all did it, we could change the world.

The theme of authenticity and action in faith runs throughout the Bible, and yet it continues to be a sort of deliberate blind spot for so many of us who call ourselves followers of Jesus. One thing is for sure: God is not fooled by useless fire. There will be a reckoning.

A prayer

Father, later in Isaiah 1 we read these words: '"Come now, let us reason together," says the Lord. "Though your sins are like scarlet, they shall be as white as snow."' This is your kind invitation to us, and we gladly accept the opportunity to think through the way we have been thinking and behaving, so that the fire of our worship and praise will not be useless. Forgive us for neglecting those who need justice and support. Show me what I can do to represent your practical love to the world. I pray that my eyes will be open to the needs of the world.

—————————— ❖ ——————————

RUNNING AHEAD

Many deceivers, who do not acknowledge Jesus Christ as coming in the flesh, have gone out into the world. Any such person is the deceiver and the antichrist. Watch out that you do not lose what you have worked for, but that you may be rewarded fully. Anyone who runs ahead and does not continue in the teaching of Christ does not have God; whoever continues in the teaching has both the Father and the Son. If anyone comes to you and does not bring this teaching, do not take him into your house or welcome him. Anyone who welcomes him shares in his wicked work.

2 JOHN 7–11

I have read one phrase in this passage many times without stopping to consider its meaning. John talks about people who 'run ahead'. It's an interesting image. Our children sometimes did it when we went out for country walks. As they grew older and their confidence increased, one or other of them would literally run on ahead and out of sight of Bridget and me, anxious to demonstrate that they were not little any more, and they did know the right way to go without being told by grown-ups. In fact, the only time I ever smacked my oldest son, Matthew, was when he persistently ran ahead in the country lanes of Norfolk where we used to live. Bridget and I made a policy decision that, in the interests of safety, I should administer one small smack on the side of Matthew's leg, and that is exactly what I did. Both Matthew and I were horrified by this dismal event, but at least he stopped running ahead.

I have no distinct memories of what happened with the other children but I seem to recall that these adventures usually ended with the distant, plaintive cry of a child who knows he is lost and needs his mum and dad more than he thought.

Perhaps the people John is talking about start in the same way. They begin by following Jesus, but, like many others in the history of the faith, they finally weary of their Master's painstaking care for each individual in each situation, and his total lack of interest in any reward that the world has to offer. They push on ahead excitedly, full of dynamic ideas and driven by the impetus of their own initiative, still using his name but unaware that they are wasting their time. Because some worldly successes can appear just the same as spiritual ones, these people seem to be flourishing for quite a long time. They acquire their own followers, admirers who help them to feel vindicated and affirmed in their great plans. Anyone who produces a word of caution or directly contradicts the inspired one is quietly removed from the equation. The end is inevitable: one day these people will stop and look around with wild, frightened eyes. Realizing that they are hopelessly lost, they will cry like children for the one they left behind, the one who knows, and indeed is, the only true way.

I ought to add that this is a very easy but subtle trap for all of us to fall into if we are not careful. I can tell you from experience that if you ever arrive at the point where you have a feeling that you and God are in cahoots and the rest of the world is getting it all wrong, then the time has come to bring yourself to a grinding halt. Jettison the God who so mysteriously agrees with everything you think and say, and retrace your steps to the place where you last encountered the real God, the one who actually exists. Life may be more challenging and less exclusive, but running ahead can only end in tears.

A prayer

Lord Jesus, keep us close to you and help us not to get carried away by our own grandiose ideas about what we and everyone else should or should not be doing. We pray for your mercy on those of us who have run ahead. We want to be with you. Give us the wisdom and courage to retreat into your care. Thank you for your willingness to take us back. We will try not to run ahead in future.

✤

DREAMS AND DRUNKENNESS

'Be careful, or your hearts will be weighed down with dissipation, drunkenness and the anxieties of life, and that day will close on you suddenly like a trap. For it will come on all those who live on the face of the whole earth. Be always on the watch, and pray that you may be able to escape all that is about to happen, and that you may be able to stand before the Son of Man.'

LUKE 21:34–36 (TNIV)

Have any of your dreams come true? I do hope so. Some of mine have. The moment when I held my first book and saw that the name on the cover really was my own—that was pretty special. I remember weighing it in my hand, flicking through the pages, trying it in various prominent positions on the bookcase, and then leaving it casually on the coffee table so that I could stroll in and out, 'noticing' that it was there. It was all very childlike, but I couldn't help it. I was so excited.

Sometimes these dreams of ours are like games. It can be great fun to discuss and picture their fulfilment, even if we suspect that they will never actually come true. It was like that with my friend

John Hall and me when Bridget and I shared a house with him in Bromley. John and I were both great admirers of the writer and broadcaster, Malcolm Muggeridge. Fewer and fewer younger people remember that name now, but for many decades this man had been everywhere, met everybody and commented on everything with style, wit and the kind of acerbic edge that can repel or attract with equal force. Muggeridge wrote like an angel, particularly perhaps in the three books that constitute his autobiography, and it was of particular interest to us that he had recently become a Christian and been formally received into the Roman Catholic Church.

'Wouldn't it be great,' John and I used to say to each other, 'if Malcolm Muggeridge could come and have tea with us in our little semi-detached house in Bromley? We could get answers to all the questions we've stored up. He'd probably enjoy it. Why don't we invite him! I bet he'd come.'

Perhaps he would have come, but as neither of us ever did get round to asking him, we were never to know. Our little dream faded. Less than a decade later, however, I did have tea with Malcolm Muggeridge (sorry you weren't there, John!) and it was then that this passage from Luke's Gospel came under discussion and a blind spot was revealed. As a matter of fact, it was his blind spot rather than mine, and it was connected with the repentant mode that seemed to be dominating his life now that he was into his 80s.

The whole thing came about because, at that time, Bridget and I were appearing regularly on the TVS television programme *Company*, which aired late at night and involved a regular pool of contributors as well as the occasional special guest. On the following day, Muggeridge was to be our guest as we recorded seven programmes in the studio. He and his wife Kitty had invited the producer and those of us who were also contributing to have tea at his house in Robertsbridge so that we could discuss the content of the programmes.

I pretended to be taking it in my stride, but it was deeply satisfying to be there and to see that little dream of mine fulfilled after all these years. As we sipped our tea and glanced around the low-ceilinged sitting-room, Bridget and I noticed photographs of Malcolm with

Mother Teresa (a major influence in his conversion), Malcom with the Pope, Malcolm, in fact, standing smilingly beside any number of 20th-century icons. Our host and hostess had welcomed us with great warmth, but they did seem very old and slightly confused. Neither of them, for instance, seemed to have quite grasped whether these programmes were to be on the radio or the television. As soon as we began to discuss plans for the following day, however, it became clear that Malcolm's mind was as keen as ever. He particularly wanted to talk about the spiritual revolution in his life.

'One night I was in a bedroom where I should never have been,' he said in those resonant, almost painfully meticulous tones that had become so well known to audiences over the years, 'and I looked in the mirror, and I saw the face of the devil, and it was my face.'

Much of his life, he went on to say, had been spent walking around European cities in a drunken haze. In fact, sex, drink and work had filled his life pretty well to the exclusion of any moral considerations.

'That's interesting,' I replied, actually venturing to say something, 'because Jesus more or less lists those three things as being most likely to distract us and draw us away from real safety, doesn't he? Debauchery, alcohol and cares of the world.'

The great man stared piercingly at me for a moment from beneath beetling brows before speaking. 'There is no point in the Gospels where Jesus specifically mentions over-indulgence in alcohol as a problem.'

This was said with such authority and conviction that I almost caved in. This was Malcolm Muggeridge, for goodness' sake! One of the greatest social commentators of the age. A few years ago he had written a book on the life of Jesus. Was it really likely that he had failed to notice a reference so relevant to himself? Well, for whatever reason, he was wrong. I showed him the verses and he nodded with surprise and humble gravitas.

Jesus does indeed mention drunkenness in these verses from Luke, and I have been interested to note how many other people are taken aback when the reference is pointed out to them. Why should that be? I have no idea why Muggeridge had failed to register something so specific, but perhaps, for most people, the answer lies in that very specificity. Drunkenness lies at the centre of Jesus' list of the three most negative influences that can affect men and women, and that fact can make us very uncomfortable. A completely un-repentant lover of good wine myself, I have to concede that our modern Christian culture, tending as usual to run parallel with general trends in society, allows us a great deal of leeway with the use and abuse of alcohol. As we have seen, Jesus flagged up the issue in no uncertain terms. I do not believe that there is anything intrinsically wrong with drinking, but I suspect that excess means different things for each of us, and, as this passage indicates, it really can be dangerous on both a physical and a spiritual level.

There are other sins, of course. Pride is one that I am sometimes prone to. I went to tea with Malcolm Muggeridge—and I corrected him!

Praise

Thank you, Father, for the public example of people like Malcolm Muggeridge, who have moved from atheism to faith, turning from their sins in repentance just as the prodigal son did. Thank you that all we prodigals will meet at your home one day. And we especially pray for those who are wrestling with drink or drug problems, that they will find help to break free and find refuge and peace in the good things of God.

✤

A BRIGHT AND BOUNCY BABY

While Peter was still speaking these words, the Holy Spirit came on all who heard the message. The circumcised believers who had come with Peter were astonished that the gift of the Holy Spirit had been poured out even on the Gentiles. For they heard them speaking in tongues and praising God.

Then Peter said, 'Can anyone keep these people from being baptized with water? They have received the Holy Spirit just as we have.' So he ordered that they be baptized in the name of Jesus Christ. Then they asked Peter to stay with them for a few days.

ACTS 10:44–48

This is not so much a blind spot contained within a few words, as it is a whole idea or way of thinking. As I have already said in the 'Beyond the veil' section, we Christians do seem to feel obliged to let God off the hook constantly, especially when we are defending his failure to act appropriately when he is clearly needed, or his strange in-and-out intervention in a world that seems desperately in need of his consistent presence. I suppose we are driven to do this for at least two reasons that I can think of. One is the constraining awareness that he is perfect, and there must therefore be a rationale for everything he does or doesn't do. Surely, we tell ourselves, if we just root around for long enough, we shall unearth that reason, and then we can pass it on to unbelievers or doubting Christians.

The other reason may be that, because of a genuine regard for our heavenly Father, we naturally feel obliged to defend him at all points. All of our limited ingenuity is used in constructing arguments that will fit the facts and explain away God's apparent failure to abide by his own rules. This has been especially true in the area of divine healing. I remember a church elder saying to me that he had anointed a number of folk with oil for healing, just as the book of James recommends, but that not one of them had been healed. 'God says through the Bible that they will be healed,' he said rather sadly, 'so that's that. I believe it. So I go on doing all the things that the Bible says I should do, all the laying on of hands and anointing with oil and everything. The trouble is that they just don't seem to get healed. I try to find explanations, but I'm running out of reasons to offer people for why it doesn't work.'

This faithful, disappointed man is not alone. Many people have

112

been through exactly the same process. There are more reasons put forward for healing 'not working' than there are books of the Bible.

Here is my suggestion in this whole matter. On reflection, I do not believe that God wants to be let off the hook. He does not want to be let off our hook, or the world's hook, or anyone else's hook. He will do what he will do, and he will not do what he will not do, and that is that. His reasons are his own business, and interesting though it would undoubtedly be to share them, it is up to him in the end.

This line of thinking was triggered for me by this passage from Acts, because it took me back to the 1960s, when it was almost an article of faith with us young Christians that you didn't need to experience anything at the point of conversion. We were so dog-matic about this. Perhaps it was because, in those days, we tended to regard faith as something that you achieved by straining hard with all the muscles of your mind. The Bible appeared to promise that the Holy Spirit would live in us when we asked Jesus into our hearts, and therefore he certainly would, even if we felt exactly the same after the prayer as before. Not believing this would reveal a lack of faith, and if our faith was lacking—well, no wonder we weren't experiencing anything.

Is your head spinning? Mine was. Silly, isn't it? But, you see, we were so anxious not to put people off or disappoint them that we defended God's failure to do anything very dynamic before he had even had a chance to not do it, if you see what I mean.

Now, of course I allow that there is much more than a germ of truth in the notion that God keeps his promises without needing firework displays, but as I read this account of the conversion of Cornelius I can't help thinking that the pendulum has, as usual, swung way too far in one direction. Partly because of some twittish teaching in the 1960s and '70s about speaking in tongues being essential to salvation, and partly because of our incessant drive to let God off the hook, large sections of the church seem to have thrown a very bright and bouncy baby out with the dreary old legalistic bathwater.

I am so weary of being cautious. I *really like* what happened to Cornelius and his family and friends. It excites and inspires me. It was from God. Wouldn't it be just wonderful for us to see and hear the Holy Spirit poured out on new converts in such a way that all those present are amazed by the way they praise God or speak in tongues or don't speak in tongues or whatever God decides is a good idea?

It does happen, but perhaps it doesn't happen enough. Let us allow that God might not do the expected thing, but for goodness' sake, let us not nervously rule out the possibility that he might.

A prayer

Lord God, you are sovereign. You will do whatever you wish and we are in no position to criticize your decisions. You do not want us to 'let you off the hook'. We do not need to make excuses for you; we need to trust you and to demonstrate and explain that trust to anyone who is curious about our faith. In this matter of experience at conversion, Lord, we don't want any silly play-acting or religious posturing, but we would like to see your Spirit poured out on men and women as it was poured out on Cornelius. If this is your will, then let it be so. We've got a bit dusty and rusty, Lord—wake us up!

STRANGE BUT TRUE:
UNCLASSIFIABLE
BLIND SPOTS

--- ⁘ ---

HE DID WHAT?

Jacob, however, took fresh-cut branches from poplar, almond and plane trees and made white stripes on them by peeling the bark and exposing the white inner wood of the branches. Then he placed the peeled branches in all the watering troughs, so that they would be directly in front of the flocks when they came to drink. When the flocks were in heat and came to drink, they mated in front of the branches. And they bore young that were streaked or speckled or spotted. Jacob set apart the young of the flock by themselves, but made the rest face the streaked and dark-coloured animals that belonged to Laban. Thus he made separate flocks for himself and did not put them with Laban's animals. Whenever the stronger females were in heat, Jacob would place the branches in the troughs in front of the animals so they would mate near the branches, but if the animals were weak, he would not place them there. So the weak animals went to Laban and the strong ones to Jacob. In this way the man grew exceedingly prosperous and came to own large flocks, and maidservants and menservants, and camels and donkeys.

GENESIS 30:37–43

I am reminded as I read this story of a somewhat similar cunning plan hatched by an impoverished local council down in the county of Gloucestershire where Bridget and I worked for a while. To prevent cows roaming from one area to another, they came up with the idea of employing a man to paint stripes across the road so that the cows would be deceived into thinking a cattle grid had been installed. It is very, very difficult to imagine a collection of more-or-less sane local councillors solemnly agreeing that this might offer an ideal solution to their problems. Perhaps one of them had been reading this passage about Jacob and taken it to heart. I am sure you are on the edge of your seat as you wonder whether such a brilliant ploy was successful. Well, I cannot believe you will be too surprised to learn that the cows were less bovine and probably cleverer than the council.

Jacob was doing what?!

All right, let's just calm down and think about this. Let's assume for a moment that all of us who are reading or are likely to read this passage have an unshakeable belief in the inerrancy, infallibility, and in-anything-else-you-like of scripture. Every detail is true down to the most obscure punctuation mark in the most impenetrable section of the least accessible chapter of the most boringly technical book in the Bible. Even so, we must surely pause to examine critically the means by which it is claimed that Jacob managed to breed speckled and spotted sheep. His method? Simple. When the animals mated in front of striped lengths of wood, their offspring were correspondingly marked. Hmm.

I'm sorry, but I really do find this a bit too difficult to swallow. Not the stuff about Jacob using his cunning to get one over on Laban. On the contrary, that is exactly what I would have expected from this Derek Trotter of the Old Testament. No, what bothers me is that Jacob's complicated breeding methods remind me all too much of Del Boy's ignorant and ill-judged schemes for making money on the streets of Peckham. This tricky stuff that the famously smooth man was doing with the goats and sheep—I mean, what is it all about?

Let me add that it is certainly not the case that I don't believe in miracles. I do. Honestly, I do. The virgin birth, no problem. Water into wine, piece of cake. Physical healing, no doubts at all. Coin in the mouth of the fish, it happened. Resurrection, centre of my faith. Second coming, could be due just after lunch. No, these things are fine and I tend to default to believing in them even when I try not to, but they pale into insignificance compared with the proposition that goats will be speckled or spotted because they mate in front of some arrangement of peeled branches.

This kind of gap between credulity and incredulity may sound odd, but in fact it is absolutely logical and natural. The point is well made in *The Curse of the Golden Cross*, one of G.K. Chesterton's famous *Father Brown* stories, when the little priest has expressed his doubts about the efficacy of a curse that is supposed to have its origins in the 13th century.

'Well,' said Tarrant, 'it's refreshing to find a priest so sceptical of the supernatural as all that.'

'Not at all,' replied the priest calmly; 'it's not the supernatural part I doubt. It's the natural part. I'm exactly in the position of the man who said, "I can believe the impossible, but not the improbable."'

'That's what you call a paradox, isn't it?' asked the other.

'It's what I call common sense, properly understood,' replied Father Brown. 'It really is more natural to believe a preternatural story, that deals with things we don't understand, than a natural story that contradicts things we do understand. Tell me that the great Mr. Gladstone, in his last hours, was haunted by the ghost of Parnell, and I will be agnostic about it. But tell me that Mr. Gladstone, when first presented to Queen Victoria, wore his hat in her drawing-room and slapped her on the back and offered her a cigar, and I am not agnostic at all. That is not impossible; it's only incredible. But I'm much more certain it didn't happen than that Parnell's ghost didn't appear; because it violates the laws of the world that I do understand. So it is with that tale of the curse. It isn't the legend that I disbelieve—it's the history.'

I'm afraid that I feel exactly the same about Jacob's breeding methods. I do not believe in them precisely because they violate laws that I do broadly understand. It would be easier for me to believe that God, in his faithfulness, organized a junior and highly embarrassed angel to go out with a divine paintpot and paintbrush every night during the lambing season, thus ensuring that Jacob got his speckled and spotted sheep, but only because the Creator was willing to give a little supernatural boost to his ridiculous plans.

The trouble with me saying all this so emphatically, of course, is that this book is bound to be read by some professor of animal psychology and husbandry who will immediately write to me with a list of well-documented cases where precisely such an effect has been brought about by precisely such means. Well, I'll just have to cross that embarrassing bridge when I come to it. In the meantime, I remain at the very least agnostic, and everyone else can, of course, believe exactly what they wish.

A prayer

Thank you, Father, for giving us access to the highly interesting and inspiring story of Jacob and all the twists and turns by which he negotiated the path of his life. Please forgive me if I am wrong about the goats and sheep, but I would need a very special and really quite glaringly vivid revelation before there could be any chance of me changing my mind. Help us, Father, to retain a sense of humour and proportion as we read the Bible, to be thankful for every part of it, but not to become slaves to the detail of some scriptural straitjacket that traps us instead of setting us free. Send us more Father Browns, we pray.

❖

THE TROUBLE WITH MARRIAGE

I would like you to be free from concern. An unmarried man is concerned about the Lord's affairs—how he can please the Lord. But a married man is concerned about the affairs of this world—how he can please his wife—and his interests are divided. An unmarried woman or virgin is concerned about the Lord's affairs: her aim is to be devoted to the Lord in both body and spirit. But a married woman is concerned about the affairs of this world—how she can please her husband. I am saying this for your own good, not to restrict you, but that you may live in a right way in undivided devotion to the Lord.

I CORINTHIANS 7:32–35

When you've been brought up as a Christian to believe that scripture is inspired to the extent that someone might easily be converted by a semicolon in Leviticus, it's difficult to *see* familiar verses, let alone disagree with them. This can make Bible reading a barren experience, which is certainly not what God wants. We are to engage with scripture, not suck it like a thumb for flavourless comfort.

Here is an example. I don't agree at all with the dogmatic statements Paul is making here. His cultural context is very different from ours. Perhaps the Corinthians really were devoted to God when they were single and completely distracted when they married, but contemporary experience seems different. Most married people I know would say that their spiritual lives have grown in authenticity through close commitment to another person, and we learn more about the fatherhood of God from the experience of parenting than any book or sermon could teach us. In addition, Christian men who have wives clever enough to know them and wise enough not to flaunt their knowledge indiscriminately have been saved from disaster and foolishness again and again by intervention that's infuriating at the time, but essential in retrospect.

Of course, Paul has a point for today's church. (I bet he's looking forward to seeing me in heaven!) Marriage and family life can become all-absorbing and distracting, just as singleness could— potentially, anyway—leave more space for exclusive service to God. But, like just about everything else in the universe, it's not as simple as that.

A prayer

Father, you will stop Paul from telling me off when I get to heaven, won't you? Seriously, I pray for all of us who try to follow Jesus, whether we are single or married. Thank you for the things you have taught me through the privilege of having a wife and children, and thank you also for teaching and blessing our single brothers and sisters. We know that you will use every one of us if we are willing. Help us to love and look after one another with warmth and understanding.

— ⸭ —

STONED AGAIN!

If someone has a stubborn and rebellious son who does not obey his father and mother and will not listen to them when they discipline him, his father and mother shall take hold of him and bring him to the elders at the gate of his town. They shall say to the elders, 'This son of ours is stubborn and rebellious. He will not obey us. He is a profligate and a drunkard.' Then all the men of his town are to stone him to death. You must purge the evil from among you. All Israel will hear of it and be afraid.
DEUTERONOMY 21:18–21 (TNIV)

Dear Pastor,

First of all, may I thank you on behalf of my husband and myself for the wonderful talk that you gave us on Sunday. In an age when standards are slipping lamentably both inside and outside the church, it was warmly encouraging to hear you take such an un-compromising stand on the inerrancy of scripture. In particular, Maurice and I appreciated your warning against the current trend for regarding the Old Testament as being in some way inferior to, or less reliable than, the New Testament—or, at the very least, a part of the Bible that needs to be approached from a wary or critical perspective. As you rightly said in your very helpful address, the whole of the Bible is directly inspired by God, and therefore we cannot simply pick and choose verses as we wish, giving credence to the sections that appeal to us and ignoring those that do not. As you explained with such eloquence, if we were to do that, then nothing, including the words of Jesus, could be relied upon.

I felt, and Maurice agreed with me, that God spoke directly to us through your words. On arriving home, I insisted that we turn off the oven and sit at the kitchen table with our Bibles, giving thanks for the wisdom of your message. Having concluded our prayer, I asked Maurice to close his eyes, open his Bible at random in the Old Testament section and place his finger on the page to see if the Lord was desiring to say something specific to us. Imagine my amazement on discovering that, through Maurice, we had been led to the passage from Deuteronomy that I have copied out at the top of this letter.

Well! Praise be! If ever the Lord spoke into a situation, it was at that moment. I was stunned and so was Maurice. It was as though those verses had been written all those years ago with our son Darren in mind. You may recall, Pastor, that Darren attended church with us until he was 14, but, sadly, has been afflicted with a spirit of rebellion for the last three years. Darren is now 17 years old, and he has become impossible to live with. He hardly works, we never know where he is at night, and he refuses either to hear what we say or to do anything that we tell him. Quite often he returns to the house in a drunken state and becomes loud and abusive if we try to remonstrate with him.

Bearing this in mind, and in view of the very specific guidance that we have received, we are determined to be obedient in this matter. To this end, I am writing to ask if we could arrange for Darren to be stoned to death, preferably at some point during the next fortnight, as we have quite heavy commitments in the following month. Unfortunately, Frattlington has no gate as such, but I believe, and Maurice has agreed with me, that the patch of waste ground between Tesco and the Esso garage is a location that one might reasonably regard as a symbolic gateway to the town.

Some practical questions. Will you arrange for the other elders to be there, or do we need to approach them individually? We are happy to do this, of course, if necessary. We know how busy you are.

Next, I am presuming, and so is Maurice, that in this case 'all the men of the town' would actually mean 'all the men of the church'. We live in a secular age, and in any case we should not be unaware of cultural differences, should we? In this connection, will you give out the notice at church next Sunday in the news time, or should I ask Maurice to do it? I expect lots of the women will ask why they can't be included, just as they always do with the men's breakfasts!

In the matter of the stones themselves, we would much appreciate your advice. Our local garden centre does offer quite nice bags of rocks at a reasonable price, but is a particular shape or size or colour more spiritually fitted for the purpose? We are novices in this field and would value your guidance.

Refreshments appropriate? Easily organized if so.

One last point: I consider, and Maurice has agreed with me, that it might be better not to tell Darren what we are planning until much nearer the date of the stoning. Do you agree?

Thank you once more for your inspiring words at the Sunday service, and for your attention to our requirements. I must go now as I have just glanced through the window to see Maurice coming up the garden path looking a little grim, and accompanied by two men I have never met before, both of them dressed in white. It reminds me just a little, pastor, of that wonderful scene after the ascension. Perhaps they are angels.

Yours in his grip…

A prayer

Lord, this is a silly exaggeration, but we do know that people can sometimes get very carried away with a slavish and inappropriate adherence to every word of the Bible. Once more we thank you for the profound richness of scripture, and we pray for wisdom, common sense and the assistance of the Holy Spirit in interpreting and comprehending the truths that you want to teach us.

BOILING WITH FURY ·

The Lord said to Moses, 'When you return to Egypt, see that you perform before Pharaoh all the wonders I have given you the power to do. But I will harden his heart so that he will not let the people go. Then say to Pharaoh, "This is what the Lord says: Israel is my firstborn son, and I told you, 'Let my son go, so he may worship me.' But you refused to let him go; so I will kill your firstborn son."'

At a lodging place on the way, the Lord met Moses, and was about to kill him. But Zipporah took a flint knife, cut off her son's foreskin and touched Moses' feet with it. 'Surely you are a bridegroom of blood to me,' she said. So the Lord let him alone.

EXODUS 4:21–26

In 40 years of services and meetings, I cannot recall one reference to the second paragraph of this passage. Not surprising, really. What is this about? Why would God select Moses to liberate Israel and then plan to kill him before he does it? And why did this unspeakable action performed by his wife prevent it from happening?

From a human perspective, I can see exactly why God might have felt like killing Moses. His response to being offered the privilege of leading a nation out of exile had been lukewarm to say the least— one long moan.

He was inadequate. He didn't know what to call God. What if the Israelites didn't believe him? He was slow of speech and tongue. Couldn't God send someone else instead?

The Bible says that God's anger burned against Moses after this Eeyore-like performance. Did God boil over with fury and decide to cut his losses and start again?

No, that can't be the answer, can it? God can't be that much like me.

The reference books say that Moses' wife, objecting to her son's circumcision, had hindered Moses in performing a rite that was closely connected with the Abrahamic covenant and the redemption of Israel. As the appointed deliverer, Moses was therefore in danger of being cut off for his sin. So Zipporah circumcised the baby with accompanying rituals and all was well.

That explanation may satisfy you. You may even understand it. If so, that's fine. I don't, and I prefer the first one.

A thought

One day we shall be able to ask for enlightenment.

✢

PROBLEMS WITH PRINCIPLES

By the word of the Lord one of the sons of the prophets said to his companion, 'Strike me with your weapon,' but the man refused.

So the prophet said, 'Because you have not obeyed the Lord, as soon as you leave me a lion will kill you.' And after the man went away, a lion found him and killed him.

The prophet found another man and said, 'Strike me, please.' So the man struck him and wounded him. Then the prophet went and stood by the road waiting for the king.

I KINGS 20:35–38a

Here is a peculiar moment from the Old Testament, one I never stopped to consider before. It all seems grossly unfair, doesn't it? Some junior prophet, empowered by God, instructs a companion to wound him, presumably with his sword. In the next few verses, we learn that this voluntary injury will be a visual aid in communicating the Lord's anger to Ahab, but did the companion understand that? Was it explained? You can hardly blame the poor bloke for being reluctant to draw blood from a prophet. Had his master gone raving mad, ordering people to stick swords in him and then threatening them with lions when they refused? Sadly, the subsequent learning curve was horribly steep and abruptly terminated.

The second man—either because he heard about the fate of the first, or perhaps because the prophet was more polite this time—did what was required, and the visual parable went ahead as planned.

Bizarre, isn't it, and, like many Old Testament stories, difficult to equate with God as revealed to us in the Gospels. As usual, I would recommend using Jesus as the lens through which to view these awkward Old Testament moments, but you may disagree with me. Please feel free.

Having said all that, I note a quite important lesson or principle in this story. It might be expressed as the proposition that virtues can be greater obstacles to obedience than sins. Sometimes (and I have experienced this myself) God wants us to do things that go against our established personal standards of behaviour, even though those standards are, in themselves, laudable and even godly. I wrote a line in a poem once that talked about the need to 'lay our cherished certainties like sad surrendered weapons at his injured feet', and I truly believe this to be necessary. It is so very hard to do, though. For some reason, I am particularly conscious of this requirement in the Communion service, when I walk to the front of the church to join the line of folk waiting to receive bread and wine. I once tried to put it into words:

Communion brings me joy, but it also makes me sad for the far less worthy but no less important reason that it demands, over and over again, my assent to the proposition that the whole of my world and my ways, negative and positive, must be left with Bible, hymnbook and spectacles on my chair as I approach to receive the bread and wine, those wonderful, rich, earthy symbols of heavenly, unearned salvation. Yes, as one of the Anglican prayers of humble access puts it, his love compels us to come in, but for some of us, there is a little death to die every single time we yield to that compulsion. Like Simon Peter centuries ago, we yet again instinctively move to draw the sword of our own will and attributes, only to feel the gentle but firmly restraining pressure of his hand upon our arm. At that same moment we hear his voice softly telling us that if we cannot come with hands that are as empty of virtues as they are of sins, we cannot come at all.

FROM *STRESS FAMILY ROBINSON 2: THE BIRTHDAY PARTY*, ZONDERVAN, 1999

Everything is provisional but Jesus. The man who never enters a pub on principle may be needed in the Red Lion on Thursday. The woman who prides herself on never being anything but polite might be required to give a mouthful to a worthy recipient. Someone who interprets good stewardship as holding on to their money could be told to stump up on the spot. Anything could happen, and I'm afraid quite a lot of it will if we are truly open to the initiatives of the Spirit. I wonder what you and I might be asked to say or do? I doubt it will involve swords, but you never know.

A prayer

Father, teach us the need to have a very light hold on anything that does not come directly from you. We are continually trying to establish ways of being and behaving that will keep us organized and safe, but we know you want us to place everything, good and bad, at your feet and at your disposal. This is not easy for some of us. Thank you for your help.

------------- ✛ -------------

THE BEAR NECESSITIES

From there Elisha went up to Bethel. As he was walking along the road, some youths came out of the town and jeered at him. 'Go on up, you baldhead!' they said. 'Go on up, you baldhead!' He turned around, looked at them and called down a curse on them in the name of the Lord. Then two bears came out of the woods and mauled forty-two of the youths. And he went on to Mount Carmel and from there returned to Samaria.

2 KINGS 2:23–25

What is supposed to be happening here? Let me get this straight. Hordes of kids pour out of the town and give a load of cheek to a slaphead prophet. Cursing them brings two bears rampaging out of the woods to sort the little perishers out. What?!

It's a familiar story, of course, but I think my recent trip to Canada made me look at it closely for the first time. Bears roam wild in Canada. I actually saw a brown bear in the far distance, although it creeps closer and closer the more frequently I tell the story. Grizzly bears, the biggest, fiercest variety, sometimes come down into town to raid garbage bins. There are leaflets telling you what to do if one attacks you. You can either lie down and remain motionless, or you can walk slowly backwards, removing articles of clothing as you go. Neither ploy appeals to me. My query is simple. Can I confidently assume that my particular bear will have read those pamphlets?

Evidently, the mouthy youths in this passage had no access to helpful pamphlets, because 42 were injured. Forty-two! How many of them were there in the first place if so many failed to escape? Eighty? A hundred? No wonder Elisha felt threatened. Where had they all come from? Why were they there? Had they nothing better to do than indulge in mass mickey-taking? If it comes to that, what sort of super-athletic wild creatures were these bears to be able to extend their mauling activities to 42 highly mobile, healthy young individuals? That's 21 each, for goodness' sake!

I suppose it shows that my mother was right. You should never make negative comments about other people's looks, especially when they have enough influence to cut short someone else's picnic in the woods.

A prayer

Father, in your wisdom you placed this story in the Bible. Why?

---- ⁜ ----

THE DANGERS OF DROPPING OFF

On the first day of the week we came together to break bread. Paul spoke to the people and, because he intended to leave the next day, kept on talking until midnight. There were many lamps in the upstairs room where we were meeting. Seated in the window was a young man called Eutychus, who was sinking into a deep sleep as Paul talked on and on. When he was sound asleep, he fell to the ground from the third storey and was picked up dead. Paul went down, threw himself on the young man and put his arms around him. 'Don't be alarmed,' he said. 'He's alive!' Then he went upstairs again and broke bread and ate. After talking until daylight, he left. The people took the young man home alive and were greatly comforted.

ACTS 20:7–12

I include this passage for two reasons. The first is that I have always been intrigued by the question of what happened when Eutychus arrived home that night. Did his wife or his mother ask him what sort of an evening he had had at the famous Christian teacher's talk, and did he reply that it had been all right except for one brief episode when he had dozed off, fallen out of the upstairs window and been killed? How easy did the folks at home find it to accept his subsequent explanation that the apostle himself had brought him back to the land of the living with some sort of spiritual bear hug? We've all heard of people finding it difficult to communicate spiritual experiences to loved ones, but this is something else! They might have been just a tad sceptical, don't you think?

Some years ago, I wrote a sketch on this very subject for use in a Bible Society revue. It features several characters who do not appear in the biblical account. Priscilla is our hero's mother and Chloe is his wife. Jason and Demus are friends of Eutychus who have also attended Paul's meeting. The action opens as Priscilla enters the house of Chloe and Eutychus, having received a message that some kind of crisis is occurring.

Priscilla: *(Offstage)* Is she in here? *(Enters)*

Chloe: Oh, Priscilla, I'm so glad you're here—I've been worried out of my mind.

Priscilla: Well, so that wretched girl of yours said, but she wouldn't say why. *(Holds her at arm's length and looks at her)* Now you just calm yourself, sit down here, and tell me what's going on. No hurry—take your time.

Chloe: It—it's Euty… *(She pronounces it 'Yooty')*

Priscilla: Eutychus? What's the matter with Eutychus? He's here, isn't he? The dawn's only just come up.

Chloe: That's just it! He's *not* here.

Priscilla: Not here? Chloe, what do you mean?

Chloe: The thing is—I don't know if Euty's told you about this job he's just started with his friend Jason down at the marble works. They work half the day each and—

Priscilla: Oh, dear! Beware of Greeks sharing shifts. That's what my old mum used to say. Came to blows over divvying up the drachmae, did they, Chloe, dear?

Chloe: Oh, no, no, the job's going really well. It's just…

Priscilla: *(Coaxingly)* Yes?

Chloe: *(Builds to a crescendo)* Well, the two of them were working together yesterday—some big order came up apparently, so everybody got called in—and afterwards they said they were going to try to drag Demus away from his market stall, and all go off to a—well, I'm not sure what it was, a sort of big religious meeting in the middle of the city, I think Euty said. A Jewish man called Paul talking about somebody else I can't remember whose name begins with a 'J'. Anyway, none of that's important. The point is that he hasn't been back all night, and there's no sign of any of the others and no news about anything from anyone and I'm really, really worried. I really am! Euty's never ever done anything like this before. Never! *(She starts to cry again)*

Priscilla: *(Holding and patting)* Now, now, take it easy, I'm sure there's a very simple explanation if only we knew it. I mean, apart from anything else, they're *males*, aren't they? The three of them probably came out of their meeting, wandered down the road, worked their way steadily through the menu at the nearest Macedonian takeaway, drank far too much wine and ended up snoring like pigs in some doorway. They'll be back— and, if it's of any interest to you, he *has* done something like this before, but it was long before you knew him.

Chloe: *(Momentarily distracted by surprise)* He has?

Priscilla: *(Fondly reminiscing)* Yes, he has. He was just a little lad at the time, all spindly arms and legs, and we were on our holidays down in Judea. I'll never forget it because of the truly amazing excuse he came up with afterwards. Talk about a fibber! *(Shakes her head and laughs)* D'you want to hear about it?

Chloe: *(Nods like a child)* Mmmm.

Priscilla: What happened was, the little monkey insisted that he wanted to go out for a walk on his own, didn't he? Had to be on his own, or he wouldn't enjoy it, he said. Budding, blossoming independence, and all that. So his father and I talked about it and agreed that as long as he didn't go too far and was back by the afternoon, he could take a little lunch in a basket and go off by himself for an hour or so. And he went—proud as anything. Well, hours and hours later, with us worried out of our heads that some undiscerning lion had gobbled him up, independence and all, in strolls Master I-can-look-after-myself-thank-you-very-much Eutychus looking a bit tired but quite cheerful, pops his basket down on the table, and says he's sorry to have been so long, but he had to share his lunch with some people.

'Had to share your lunch with some people?' I said.

'Yes,' he said.

'How many people?' I said.

'Five thousand,' he said.

'Is that *all*?' I said.

'Well, it might have been a few more than that,' he said, 'I didn't actually count them.' (*They both laugh*) We were so glad to see him back safe and sound, we hardly got cross at all, just told him there was no need to make silly excuses, and sent him off to bed. I sat with him for a while, and do you know what?

Chloe: (*Totally absorbed by now*) What?

Priscilla: Well, I asked him what *really* happened, quite gently—you know. Did he get lost or something and feel silly about telling us?

Chloe: What did he say?

Priscilla: (*Thoughtful pause*) Funny how you forget things, isn't it? I'm pretty sure he said he'd been at some kind of preaching thing, just like this time, but the man doing the talking wasn't called Paul. Let me think… (*Pause*) Do you know, I'm almost sure Eutychus said his name began with 'J', like the one you said this Paul fellow was going to talk about last night. Now, is that a coincidence, or is that a coincidence?

Chloe: (*Shaking her head*) That's a coincidence.

Priscilla: Anyway, he stuck to his story—all excited inside, he seemed to be, I remember that—eyes shining. Told me with a dead straight face that this 'J' character had borrowed his lunch, if you please—five little loaves and two small fish it was—and broken it up to feed these five thousand people who'd been so keen to hear what 'J' had to say that they'd forgotten to take any food with them. He told me very solemnly that it took more than two hours for the man to break off enough bread and fish for everyone, and that's why he was late, because— wait for it—he knew I'd want the basket back. (*They both laugh again*) He told it so well, he almost had me believing him.

Chloe: But… what a funny story for Euty to make up.

Priscilla: (*Nods*) Funny isn't the word. Gets it from his father, I think. I don't suppose the excuse he comes in with this morning will be half as interesting. (*Both laugh. Chloe shakes her head*) But he definitely made up the lunch story. I mean, quite apart from the sheer absurdity of it all, when I went downstairs that night, I remember peeping under the cloth inside the lunch basket where he'd left it on the table, and you'll never guess what I found.

Chloe: (*Enthralled*) What?

Priscilla: Five little loaves and two small fish. They hadn't even been touched.

After a short reflective pause, Jason and Demus rush into the house looking dishevelled but very excited. Chloe and Priscilla jump to their feet.

Chloe: Jason! Demus! Where's Euty? What's happened? Why isn't he with you?

Jason: (*Throwing his arms wide and speaking as though he's announcing wonderful news*) He's been killed!

Chloe faints. All cluster noisily round to help. She slowly revives and is back on her feet before she speaks again.

Chloe: (*Fearful*) D-d-did you say Euty's been killed?

Demus: *(Enthusiastically)* Yes, he fell out of a third-floor window and broke his neck!

Chloe: Oh, no!

Priscilla: *(Aghast but in control)* Would you two young men mind explaining why you insist on announcing my son's death as if it was a cause for celebration?

Jason: Because he's not dead! He's alive!

Priscilla: *(Pause, then rather hysterically)* He's been killed but he's not dead? He had a fatal accident that resulted in him being alive? What on earth are you— *(Eutychus enters)* Eutychus!

Chloe faints again. All cluster round once more until she recovers and is seated.

Chloe: Oh, Euty, you're alive! They said you were dead.

J/E/D: *(All start speaking at once)* He was! He stopped breathing! I broke my neck! *[and so on]*

Priscilla: *(Raises a hand to silence them)* This beats the loaves and fishes into a cocked hat. Right, now, look, just tell us slowly and clearly what's been going on. Demus—you start.

Demus: Right, well, we went to hear Paul of Tarsus speak—all three of us—and it was up on the third floor of one of those tall buildings in the centre of town. The place was packed and hot, wasn't it, you chaps? *(Eutychus and Jason nod vigorously)* Jason and I sat on the floor with our backs to the wall, and Eutychus perched right on the window ledge so that he'd—you know—get the benefit of the draught. And he fell asleep, didn't you, Eut?

Eutychus: Yes, I—

Jason: We had our backs to him, you see, because we were listening to the speaker.

Demus: Great speaker—not flash or anything, but a great speaker.

Priscilla: *(Drily to her son)* Hmmm, such a great speaker that he put you to sleep, eh?

Eutychus: Well, he *was* a very interesting speaker, mother, but, I dunno—maybe there's something about this new religion that makes people go talking on and on for hours and hours.

Jason: Anyway, neither of us realized that after three or four hours old Eut had just—

Demus: Dropped off.

Jason: Literally.

Jason, Demus and Eutychus laugh uproariously but stop abruptly as they realize that Priscilla and Chloe are not amused.

Demus: Yes, well, anyway, we suddenly heard this sort of dull thump down below and when we looked out we saw that Eut had—well, he'd fallen over backwards down on to the floor of the yard. We were devastated, weren't we, Jason? *(Jason nods earnestly)* We rushed down as fast as we could, but when we got there… *(Shrugs)* he was stone dead. Weren't you, Eut?

Eutychus: So I'm told.

Chloe: Oh, Euty! Oh, my darling!

Jason: *(Seriously)* I cried. Real tears. You did too, didn't you, Demus? Howling like babies, we were. Horrible thing to happen—horrible! All blood and—oh, horrible! And—well, that was it really. That's what happened, isn't it, Demus?

Demus: Yep! Any food about?

Jason: We're starving! *(Pause as Priscilla and Chloe wait for more)*

Chloe: But… but… but… but… but…

Priscilla: (With heavy sarcasm) I think Chloe is trying to say that you might have missed out one itsy-bitsy, teensy-weensy bit of the story. The trivial little unimportant detail about how he comes to be alive now when he was so recently deceased. Forgive our vulgar curiosity, but we'd love to know.

Demus: Oh, sorry! Of course—missed out the really interesting bit. Well, I suppose Paul must have realized that no one was listening any more, so he stopped talking at last—

Jason: Great speaker, mind you.

Demus: Oh, yes, a terrific speaker—and he followed us downstairs and out to where the corp—err, where Eutychus was lying. And then, well, he sort of looked at you and me, didn't he, Jason?

Jason: Yes, we were crying by then. Real tears. And this Paul— he just kind of threw himself on the corp— on to Eutychus, and wrapped his arms round him as if... *(Searches for words)*

Demus: As if he was dragging him back from somewhere...

Pause

Jason: Then he got up—Paul, I mean—and smiled at us, and said, 'Don't worry, lads. Your friend's alive.' And—he was.

Demus: We were a bit surprised.

Jason: Yeah, we were a bit. And then we thought, well, he's alive, not a scratch on him. Let's stay for the end of the meeting.

Demus: So we did. And here we are now.

Short silence

Priscilla: *(With a mother's sudden perception)* You saw him again last night, didn't you, Eutychus? The man who borrowed your lunch all those years ago. You saw him, didn't you?

Eutychus: *(Slowly, with a faraway look in his eyes)* I don't remember anything about falling. I just remember finding myself going up this long tunnel, and he was standing at the end of it. He looked just the same. I walked right up to him and he smiled and said, 'Good to see you again. Shall I send you back, or will you come with me?' And I said, 'Whatever you say, Master.' Then he put his arms round me, and suddenly I was... awake... alive... back to normal. But... I think normal's changed. *(He embraces Chloe)*

Priscilla: *(Decisively)* Jason, Demus, Eutychus, sit yourselves down. Right, you three, I'll organize something for us all to eat and drink, and then Chloe and I want to hear everything—and I mean *everything* you know—about this man whose name begins with 'J'.

I don't know how the conversation would have developed after that, but I am very interested by Luke's comment about the people taking their friend home and being greatly comforted. Leaving aside the obvious fact that they were relieved and consoled by his unexpected revival, it occurs to me that they probably experienced a kind of comfort that we sorely need today. To put it bluntly, they had discovered that Paul was not just a load of talk. When disaster happened, his response was neither abstract nor theoretical. It was a vigorous blend of the practical and spiritual, resulting in a solution that underlined and confirmed the reality of the Christian truths that he had been teaching to the people of Troas.

How we need that blend of truth and action in our churches.

A prayer

Lord, give us the courage and the faith to turn theory into practice. Perhaps we cannot all be like Paul, but we can dedicate ourselves more exclusively to your service. We want to see more of our brothers and sisters bringing practical healing and help to the world at the same time as they offer the words of life. Not silly games, Lord, but genuine demonstrations of your compassion and power in a world that needs you so much. We yearn to see people come to you because they witness the way in which you work through your servants. Teach us how to be helpful in making that happen, Lord. Thank you.

✣

LUNCH-TIME LAUGHS
AND ELIJAH THE COMEDIAN

The apostles gathered around Jesus and reported to him all they had done and taught. Then, because so many people were coming and going that they did not even have a chance to eat, he said to them, 'Come with me by yourselves to a quiet place and get some rest.'

So they went away by themselves in a boat to a solitary place. But many who saw them leaving recognized them and ran on foot from all the towns and got there ahead of them. When Jesus landed and saw a large crowd, he had compassion on them, because they were like sheep without a shepherd. So he began teaching them many things.

By this time it was late in the day, so his disciples came to him. 'This is a remote place,' they said, 'and it's already very late. Send the people away so they can go to the surrounding countryside and villages and buy themselves something to eat.'

But he answered, 'You give them something to eat.'

MARK 6:30–37

Elijah said to the prophets of Baal, 'Choose one of the bulls and prepare it first, since there are so many of you. Call on the name of your god, but do not light the fire.' So they took the bull given them and prepared it.

Then they called on the name of Baal from morning till noon. 'O Baal, answer us!' they shouted. But there was no response; no one answered. And they danced around the altar they had made.

At noon Elijah began to taunt them. 'Shout louder!' he said. 'Surely he is a god! Perhaps he is deep in thought, or busy, or travelling. Maybe he is sleeping and must be awakened.' So they shouted louder and slashed themselves with swords and spears, as was their custom, until their blood flowed. Midday passed, and they continued their frantic prophesying until the time for the evening sacrifice. But there was no response, no one answered, no one paid attention.

I KINGS 18:25–29

Because I sometimes try to bring a smile to the faces of my readers and listeners, I am often asked if there are examples of humour in the Bible. Some ask the question quite innocently and because they really would like to know. Others, I suspect, are hoping to make a case for their view that humour is 'not helpful' to those who are trying to take the Christian faith seriously. Well, of course, the Bible as a whole is not exactly a bundle of laughs, but I usually point out one or two instances of humour, some obvious, others more subtle. I am reliably informed by a Jewish scholar of the New Testament that many aspects of the parables of Jesus would have had them rocking in the aisles. You had to be there, I guess.

One moment that has always amused me is the occasion recorded above in Mark's Gospel, when five thousand people needed to be fed. As we can see, the disciples have returned excitedly from their first missionary trip and are absolutely full of all that they have done and seen. Jesus suggests a period of rest in a quiet place, but the plan is thwarted as usual by the arrival of a huge crowd. The day wears on. People are hungry. The disciples, full of confidence after their powerful experience of ministry, know just what should be done and advise Jesus accordingly. Have you ever asked yourself what his reply to them could possibly mean?

'You give them something to eat.'

No wonder they were surprised. Did he really think that they had access to enough food for five thousand hungry people, or sufficient money to pay for it? No, my guess is that Jesus was gently putting a brake on the acceleration of his disciples' positive view of themselves. They had seen miracles happening while they were away.

Perhaps, quite naturally, they had begun to believe that these marvels were more to do with them than with the Holy Spirit.

'OK,' Jesus is saying, 'you lot are great healers and miracle workers. Here's a crowd of hungry people. Why don't you use some of your amazing power to feed them?' Did he smile? Did they smile? Did God smile? It makes me smile.

Then we come to the passage from the first book of Kings. I include this extract from the fascinating story of the great prophet because it contains an element I have failed to notice in the past. Let me explain.

This, clearly, was not the best of days for the prophets of Baal, especially as their frantically praying, self-mutilating nightmare ended with every last one of them being slaughtered. A horrible end to the affair, but definitely game, set and match to God and Elijah. The thing that strikes me is that, at this stage of the story, we have Elijah doing a short but pithy Blackadderish bit of stand-up comedy at the expense of the prophets of Baal and for the benefit of the onlookers. Perhaps Baal is so wrapped up in his thoughts, suggests Elijah, that he has shut out the voices of all his prophets. Or maybe he's got some important job on and can't get away. Could he be on his holidays? Or is it just that Baal is fast asleep and they haven't made sufficient noise to wake him? The humour is dark and searingly sarcastic, but read it again. It really is funny.

The Bible is not a joke book, and the literary conventions of the time do not seem to allow for much humour of the kind that we would understand, but we men and women are made in the image of God, and our sense of humour is a valuable part of us. Jesus was a real man, and I am sure that there were times, in the midst of a great deal of sorrow, when he just had to laugh. And when that happened, how the company of heaven must have laughed with him.

A prayer

Father, we know that you weep, and so do we. But you also like to laugh, and so do we. We will tell you some of our reasons for laughing, and you tell us some of yours. Oh, and Father, I would just love to have been there to see Jesus laugh.

A CARING GOD

---- ❖ ----

THE PEACE OF GOD
AND THE GIFT OF ANGELS

'You believe at last!' Jesus answered. 'But a time is coming, and has come, when you will be scattered, each to his own home. You will leave me all alone. Yet I am not alone, for my Father is with me.

'I have told you these things, so that in me you may have peace. In this world you will have trouble. But take heart! I have overcome the world.'
JOHN 16:31–33

What does Jesus mean? Why put two apparently contradictory statements side by side as though one explains the other? First of all, Jesus says, we will have trouble in this world. Got it. Next, he declares that he has overcome the world. OK, got that too. But in that case, why will we have trouble? What does 'overcoming' mean if things continue to go wrong?

Instead of vaguely assuming that someone else has resolved the paradox so we need not bother, let's try to understand.

No problem with the first part. We do have troubles. Some are problems that Christians and non-Christians routinely face: bereavement, sickness, poverty and depression. Some are directly related to faith. Not too long ago, a church member was subjected to a frighteningly aggressive verbal attack in the high street of our town. It's far from martyrdom, I know, but we can sense that such things, and worse, will happen more and more in this country over the next few years. We know that in other countries thousands of people do face actual martyrdom every year.

So, yes, we know troubles, but in what sense has Jesus overcome the world in which they happen? How can we have the peace that he speaks of in the midst of such tumult?

My answer to this question, the only one I have, is sad, beautiful, challenging and frightening. In one sense, it makes us into aliens and sojourners. It separates us from the source of our being and changes for ever our definition of 'home'. The fact is that ultimate peace can only be found in him. We must abandon all other reference points and trust that he has overcome the power that the devil once had over the souls of men and women. Nothing can harm us if we are in him, and the relationship will last for eternity.

Fine wine or vinegar? The peace of the Lord or the peace of the world? Not an easy choice. Which will we pursue? Of course, Jesus himself fought this battle out during those 40 uncomfortable days spent in the wilderness, and, after successfully withstanding the devil's oleaginous ploys, he was ministered to by angels. It may be a source of comfort for some who are reading these words and yearning for the peace that comes from God to know that similar experiences are not wholly unknown in this age. There are many different kinds of desert and more than one variety of angelic ministry. One in particular springs to mind.

I was sitting on the front row of a chapel in a conference centre thousands of miles from home in a country that I had never visited before. In a few minutes I would be getting to my feet and speaking to the people who were assembled there.

Landing in this place had been a nightmare. The pilot seemed to be deliberately flying straight into the centre of the most crowded part of the city. The illusion was dispelled, thank God, but only at the last moment.

Unbelievably, I had flown all those miles folded into the instrument of torture that we call an economy airline seat, just to lead a church weekend. After spending a few pleasant days unfolding my body and recovering from jetlag in the city, this morning I had been transported by ferry, together with members of the church, from the mainland to the island where the weekend was to be based. There was no mechanical transport allowed on this island, and the journey from the jetty where the ferry tied up involved a long, winding, climbing, luggage-burdened walk in the humid atmosphere that typified weather in that part of the world. Before leaving sea level, my heart had lifted as I noticed one or two simple but extremely seductive seafood restaurants. If any free time became available, I looked forward to coming back down that hill, unencumbered, so that I could taste some authentic oriental cooking. To misquote the famous West End musical number, 'Food, food changes everything…'

Now, all our belongings had been deposited in a selection of adequate but spartan rooms, we had eaten a good meal, and the first formal session of the weekend was about to begin. It would include my opening address to the church members. All the people I had met had been very encouraging and friendly and nice, but a cold hand was gripping my heart as I prepared to speak for the first time. I never had been very good at being away from home and family. Experience has shown me that the darkest of these feelings pass as soon as I actually get going; otherwise I would have had to stop this madness long ago. In the meantime, however, I felt as I did when I was a small boy of seven, sitting miserably at a wooden desk in my new school in Miss Buchanan's class, wishing that my mummy could come and take me home. Pathetic! When would I grow up and deal with these things in a more mature way?

'Lord, help me,' I prayed, 'because my heart is failing inside me.'

Suddenly a cool hand was laid on one of mine, and then another. Angels? I looked up. Two little girls I had noticed earlier but not yet spoken to—daughters of a couple from the church—were standing at my knee, gazing solemnly into my eyes. They smiled very slightly, but offered no explanation at all for leaving their seats at the back to come and be with me for a few moments. They were just there. So still. How very strange that they should do this, I thought. Had anyone suggested that they should come to the front, or had they done it of their own accord? It really did not matter. They were so serene and so relaxed and so unequivocally present with me that my discomfort was eased. I could feel the tension go from my face, and especially from my jaw, which often tightens when the pressure is on. It was such a privilege to be comforted by children. Jesus spoke to me through his apprenticed angels. 'No shame at all in feeling that you are like one of these,' he said.

It was exactly the kind of peace and comfort I needed in my own trivial little desert, and I thanked him for it.

A prayer

Lord, we seek the greater peace that is in you, and we ask you to strengthen our resolve when the desert seems too hot and too uncomfortable to bear. We know in our hearts that your peace is deeper and more empowering than anything the world has to offer, but there are times when it would be much easier to give in. Thank you for sending your angels to help us, even if we don't always recognize them.

❖

GIVING IN AND NOT GIVING IN

That night Jacob got up and took his two wives, his two female servants and his eleven sons and crossed the ford of the Jabbok. After he had sent them across the stream, he sent over all his possessions. So Jacob was left alone, and a man wrestled with him till daybreak. When the man saw that he could not overpower him, he touched the socket of Jacob's hip so that his hip was wrenched as he wrestled with the man. Then the man said, 'Let me go, for it is daybreak.'

But Jacob replied, 'I will not let you go unless you bless me.'

The man asked him, 'What is your name?'

'Jacob,' he answered.

Then the man said, 'Your name will no longer be Jacob, but Israel, because you have struggled with God and with human beings and have overcome.'

Jacob said, 'Please tell me your name.'

But he replied, 'Why do you ask my name?' Then he blessed him there.

So Jacob called the place Peniel, saying, 'It is because I saw God face to face, and yet my life was spared.'

The sun rose above him as he passed Peniel, and he was limping because of his hip. Therefore to this day the Israelites do not eat the tendon attached to the socket of the hip, because the socket of Jacob's hip was touched near the tendon.

GENESIS 32:22–32 (TNIV)

I do feel some identification with Jacob as I write this. I suffered from a trapped nerve in my left leg for some years. Not very long after that cleared up, I managed to twist my right hip, and the pain of that injury is still with me. Neither of these afflictions occurred as a result of wrestling with God, I ought to add, but the pain is probably about the same.

This bizarre experience of Jacob's happened at what we might reasonably call a crossroads in his life, the point where his dealings with the tricky Laban were over and he was full of dread and all sorts of other emotions about encountering his brother Esau the following day for the first time in years. It is not surprising that such a night should be filled with wrestling and conflict. I have known dark and tumultuous nights like that, and so have many of you. But what was going on here? It's all so strange. What can possibly be meant by the suggestion that Jacob was actually wrestling with God? Why was the man who turned out to be God unable to overpower a mere mortal? Why did God 'cheat' in the end by touching Jacob's hip? How did Jacob know that it was God even though the man had refused to divulge his name?

Clearly it all has something to do with the establishment of Jacob's new and more substantial identity as Israel, the father of a people, and a man who had struggled with God and himself and survived. Perhaps the vigour with which Jacob fought and held on to the man who turned out to be God was a significant measure of his determination to make the Lord's blessing his number one priority for the first time in his life. The touch on the hip was merely a reminder that, in the final analysis, the master is the master.

Is there a pattern or process here that might be of use to us? Is there any circumstance or situation in which we could be said to wrestle with God and ourselves and become better or more useful people as a result? Perhaps there is a clue in Jacob's insistence that he would not release the man (a man who, being God, could have released himself at any time he wanted) until he was granted a blessing.

I am reminded of the days and weeks following the onset of a stress illness nearly 20 years ago. There certainly was a sense in which, having jettisoned most of the frills and absurdities of what I had called my faith, I wrestled against the Spirit of God every morning in prayer and with a fierce intensity of contemplation. I wanted something from God. I suppose I was almost demanding that the relationship I had always hoped for should become a reality, and I was not going to let go of him until something broke or changed or was opened or became clearly visible. And I think it was all right to behave like that. It was all right to struggle and clutch and batter and plead. I seemed to feel in my spirit that God was perfectly happy to adjust his power and strength to a level where the fight was an even one.

Anyone who engages in play-fights with their own small children will know exactly what I mean. You could win at any moment if you really wished. One blow of the fist with normal adult strength would do it, but obviously that is never how you want the contest to be ended. Granted, it might become necessary to let your small adversary know who is boss from time to time by throwing him on the sofa (or touching the socket of his hip), but the object of the exercise is to give him a better feeling about himself, to enable him to experience healthy physical intimacy, and to allow him a safe experience of battling against superior strength—in other words, to gain a blessing.

I enjoyed those mornings with God. No, more than that, I relished and valued them. They made me feel better about myself and better about my heavenly Father. And the same, I would suggest, must have been true for Jacob.

A thought

When I look back, it seems to me that I have known quite a lot of Christians who bear scars from their encounters with God, and they are invariably the better for it. There is a sense of sweet sadness about men and women who have learned to serve through strenuous engagement with the living God. They have given in and they have also not given in. As a result, they are filled with a light that is not their own.

————— ✤ —————

I'VE HAD ENOUGH

Now Ahab told Jezebel everything Elijah had done and how he had killed all the prophets with the sword. So Jezebel sent a messenger to Elijah to say, 'May the gods deal with me, be it ever so severely, if by this time tomorrow I do not make your life like that of one of them.'

Elijah was afraid and ran for his life. When he came to Beersheba in Judah, he left his servant there, while he himself went a day's journey into the desert. He came to a broom tree, sat down under it and prayed that he might die. 'I have had enough, Lord,' he said. 'Take my life; I am no better than my ancestors.' Then he lay down under the tree and fell asleep.

All at once an angel touched him and said, 'Get up and eat.' He looked around, and there by his head was some bread baked over hot coals, and a jar of water. He ate and drank and then lay down again.

The angel of the Lord came back a second time and touched him and said, 'Get up and eat, for the journey is too much for you.'

So he got up and ate and drank. Strengthened by that food, he travelled forty days and forty nights until he reached Horeb, the mountain of God.

1 KINGS 19:1–8 (TNIV)

One short phrase caught my eye as I was reading these verses about Elijah. I was hardly aware that I had noticed it until a few days later, when I was reading the book of James in the New Testament. 'Elijah,' says James in chapter 5, 'was a man just like us.'

Those were the words that made the link. I turned back to the passage above and picked out the five words that had arrested my eye a week earlier.

'I have had enough, Lord.'

There it is. Sufficient evidence, if you are anything like me, to confirm that James was right. Elijah was indeed a man—a person—just like us. Most of us have reached the point at one time or another where all we can say is that we have had enough. And for those who are in some kind of specific ministry, as Elijah was, this can be particularly hard. The helplessness of the God-driven life when God has momentarily taken his hands off the wheel is profound indeed. This Elijah, this great man of God, has just defeated the prophets of Baal in spectacular style, and now he finds himself running like a scared chicken from the threats of Jezebel. It is so hard, is it not, brothers and sisters, to reach the edge of ourselves, as we do quite frequently, and to realize that anything we have accomplished has been accomplished by God? Cause for rejoicing no doubt, but so hard sometimes, so very hard.

Take heart. Read the next few verses and see how kind God was to his despairing servant. On a very personal note, it reminds me of something my mother used to do for me. During my teenage years, I would occasionally stay out much later than the time that had been agreed with my parents. By the time I got home, all the lights in the house were off, including the one in the bedroom that I shared with my brother. I knew there would be trouble in the morning—interrogation and angry words—but I knew something else as well. I knew that if I reached my hand out as I lay in the dark, I would find a glass of milk and a little pile of Marmite sandwiches on a chair beside the bed. My mother put them there because, although she might well be angry, she never stopped loving me.

I was no prophet. I was a bad boy. But I think the feeling might have been very similar.

A prayer

Father, some of us have reached the bottom. Whether it is our fault or not, we need your kindness now. Come to us in our despair and feed us with the food we need to gain strength and go back to being useful servants for you. Thank you for people like my mother, who teach us so much about the kind of love that you offer to us.

✜

GOD WILL TORTURE US?

Then Peter came to Jesus and asked, 'Lord, how many times shall I forgive someone who sins against me? Up to seven times?'

Jesus answered, 'I tell you, not seven times, but seventy-seven times.

'Therefore, the kingdom of heaven is like a king who wanted to settle accounts with his servants. As he began the settlement, a man who owed him ten thousand bags of gold was brought to him. Since he was not able to pay, the master ordered that he and his wife and his children and all that he had be sold to repay the debt.

'The servant fell on his knees before him. "Be patient with me," he begged, "and I will pay back everything." The servant's master took pity on him, cancelled the debt and let him go.

'But when that servant went out, he found one of his fellow servants who owed him a hundred silver coins. He grabbed him and began to choke him. "Pay back what you owe me!" he demanded.

'His fellow servant fell to his knees and begged him, "Be patient with me, and I will pay you back."

'But he refused. Instead, he went off and had the man thrown into prison until he could pay the debt. When the other servants saw what had happened, they were greatly distressed and went and told their master everything that had happened.

'Then the master called the servant in. "You wicked servant," he said, "I cancelled all that debt of yours because you begged me to. Shouldn't you have had mercy on your fellow servant just as I had on you?" In anger his master handed him over to the jailers to be tortured, until he should pay back all he owed.

'This is how my heavenly Father will treat each of you unless you forgive a brother or sister from your heart.'

MATTHEW 18:21–35

There are some ghoulish Christians who seem to take a deep and unhealthy delight in pointing out the horrible things that God has promised to do to anyone who dares to step out of line or disobey him. This kind of depraved appetite can have a terribly negative effect on what one might term 'the little ones at the back'. By this I mean followers of Jesus who thought very little of themselves in the first place, and are more than ready to believe that they deserve any ghastly punishment that God cares to inflict on them. They are so easily bullied, and God hates bullying. So do I. So there!

Having said all that, we are not excused from facing and trying to understand those elements in the teaching of Jesus that appear uncompromisingly tough or even cruel. That is why I have included such a long passage from Matthew's Gospel in this collection. The blind spot itself is contained within a handful of words, but we cannot begin to make sense of it outside the context of the story that Jesus is telling, and the point he is trying to make.

The parable of the unmerciful servant is a familiar one, of course, and it answers the question that Peter—on our behalf, if you like— asks of his Master. How long, he wants to know, should we go on forgiving someone who is hurting or upsetting us? He suggests hopefully and rather plaintively that seven times might be quite sufficient. But Jesus is having none of it. 'You must go on forgiving until you are blue or red or green in the face,' he tells Peter, and he continues with a story that is designed to explain why that is so.

The master, who would have been acting entirely within his legal rights if he had thrown the servant into prison or sold him and his family into slavery, magnanimously releases the unattractive central figure in the parable from a vast debt. The recipient of this great-hearted generosity then fails to extend the same mercy to his fellow servant and ends up being tortured in the same prison that he probably avoided by the skin of his teeth in the first place. And this, says Jesus, is how his heavenly Father will treat each of us unless we forgive our brothers or sisters from the heart.

Good. Fine. Got it. That's perfectly… wait a minute! What is Jesus saying? Is he really telling us that God will punish us exactly as the ungrateful servant was punished if we fail to forgive others? Are we to be tortured if we run out of compassion after the 23rd or 79th or 96th time of asking? Tortured! What is Jesus talking about? How could a loving God even contemplate subjecting us to torture because, frail as we are, we fail to reach his perfect standards? What can it possibly mean? It's not fair! It's horrible! It's—

All right, all right, let's just calm down and consider one or two points.

First of all, it's a story. It's a little piece of fiction used to make the point that God has forgiven a world of sin, and that therefore we should be more than ready to reflect that generosity in our treatment of others. If Jesus was here in the flesh once more, I suspect that he would sigh and shake his head with frustration on learning that we habitually pick bits out of his parables and worry at them as if we were dogs with a sliver of strange-smelling bone.

The second point is about motivation. What is God's motivation in telling this story through his Son? Well, if we have learned nothing else in our travels through this strange collection of books that we call the Bible, we must surely have understood that God invariably defaults to compassion. Jonah knew this and it really annoyed him. It has annoyed many people down the years who have known *exactly* how their treasured projects should end, and have then discovered that God has his own very specific ideas.

Wherever there is a loophole for love, God will use it. This story is told for our benefit. Look at the familiar words of the Lord's Prayer, spoken by Jesus in the sixth chapter of the same Gospel.

'This, then, is how you should pray:

> *Our Father in heaven,*
> *hallowed be your name,*
> *your kingdom come,*
> *your will be done*
> *on earth as it is in heaven.*
> *Give us this day our daily bread.*
> *Forgive us our debts,*
> *as we also have forgiven our debtors.*
> *And lead us not into temptation,*
> *but deliver us from the evil one.*

'For if you forgive others when they sin against you, your heavenly Father will also forgive you. But if you do not forgive others their sins, your Father will not forgive your sins.'
MATTHEW 6:9–15 (TNIV)

There is a crucially important spiritual law laid down in these words. It dictates that if we do not forgive, we cannot be forgiven. Don't ask me why God can't break his own law if he wants to. I don't know why. I just know that he can't. Jesus is anxious that we should not suffer from the negative consequences of breaking that law, and this brings us to our third point.

Presumably the term 'torture' is used in Matthew 18 because of the cultural context, and in order to fit in with the story, but it is also clearly a warning. There is a state, perhaps simply separation from the love of God, which will be akin to torture. It will hurt and hurt for ever and ever, and Jesus and his heavenly Father do not want that for us. They passionately want us to be in heaven with them. Well, all right, but some of us find it very difficult to forgive.

For instance, there was a woman Bridget and I met after an evening talk in the Midlands recently. It began well. We performed two new sketches for the first time, always a nerve-wracking business. They seemed to work. People laughed in the right places, and we managed to keep straight faces where appropriate. It was a warm and supportive atmosphere. Our audience, mainly local church folk, nodded and smiled affirmingly as we went on to talk about the crucial need to look after each other, and to forgive each other freely when we felt we had suffered hurt. It seemed to go well, and afterwards, as we moved to the back of the hall to sign books and chat to people, we felt content. The major part of the task was over and our material had been well received.

'I hate the woman next door to me. I'm never going to forgive her.'

The first person to approach us after our talk made this statement in an unabashed, matter-of-fact tone.

'Oh, but surely—'

'She accused me of something I never did, and as far as I'm concerned, that's it. Some things you can't forgive.'

I gazed at her for a moment, nonplussed. We had just spent an hour talking about the need to love and forgive our enemies as well as our friends. Had it meant nothing to this woman?

I did try. I honestly did. I reminded her of the things Jesus said in the passage that appears above, but if ever anyone had a blind spot, this was hers. It was as though the eyes of her mind and spirit were not capable of comprehending the proposition that followers of Jesus might move beyond the place of their own, inchoate feelings, or set aside the rights granted by the world, for the sake of peace in the family of God. She was very calm. She just couldn't see it. She was blind. I pray that her sight will be restored. It rather spoiled the evening. That woman is by no means alone, though. I have had problems with forgiveness from time to time. Most of us have.

Fair enough. So, one more point.

Clearly we cannot reach the perfect standard that Jesus demands, not on this side of the grave. That is indisputably true. We do have to bear in mind one rather important little point, though: Jesus died for us. The full meaning of that phrase is a cosmos away from my understanding, but there is one thing that I do hazily comprehend. Intercession by Jesus to his Father on my behalf makes me perfect in God's sight, as long as I am confessing my shortcomings (including failure to forgive), and obediently co-operating with the Holy Spirit in finding ways to deal with my weaknesses (including failure to forgive) and move forward as far as I am able. Perhaps God is rather like the best of old-fashioned bank managers. As long as you stay in touch, something can always be worked out.

A prayer

Father, forgive us for doubting your good intentions towards us. Sometimes we lose confidence and assume that no one could possibly care enough about us to turn heaven and earth upside down so that we will be safe in the end. Thank you for releasing us from the debt that we owe you, and please help us to work hard to reflect that generosity when it comes to our relationships with those who have hurt us. It really is not easy, Father, but we know that you want us to do it, so we will try to be obedient. Thank you also that Jesus died for us so that we can face you in our imperfect state and know that we are justified because of him. You default to compassion, Father, and we are blessed because of that. Thank you.

THE DISAPPOINTMENT OF GOD

But do not forget this one thing, dear friends: With the Lord a day is like a thousand years, and a thousand years are like a day. The Lord is not slow in keeping his promise, as some understand slowness. He is patient with you, not wanting anyone to perish, but everyone to come to repentance.

But the day of the Lord will come like a thief. The heavens will disappear with a roar; the elements will be destroyed by fire, and the earth and everything in it will be laid bare.

2 PETER 3:8–10

I include this passage because recently the implication of one phrase in it jumped up and hit me between the eyes for the very first time. It vividly reveals a truth that is at once moving, humbling and puzzling. It also reminds me of a friend I have not seen for some time.

God does not want anyone to perish. Say those words out loud to yourself. 'God does not want anyone to perish.' And the implication of this statement? Simple but stunning: God is not going to be able to have what he wants. He is going to be disappointed. Chew on that thought for a moment.

I find it moving because I believe that the heart of God is very large and full of love, and he has worked so hard to make it possible for as many as possible to come home. He will wait in vain for countless numbers who have not answered the call. There will be no running down the road to meet them with cloaks and rings and fattened calves and invitations to a party. He will be heartbroken.

It is humbling because we human beings, products of his creative art, made from the dust and in his image, are the objects of this great love and the cause of the joy and disappointment that are to come.

It is puzzling for all the old reasons that we cannot help expressing, whatever anyone says. If God really is all-powerful and all-loving, why can he not stretch a point and let them all in? Please don't bother to write and fill me in on the theological basis for exclusion. I know the party line. I just feel very sorry for God.

The friend I was reminded of is a woman of advanced years, a secondary school teacher all her life, who never married and has now retired to live in a small village in Cornwall. Margaret has been a Christian for as long as she can remember. Her faith lights up her life as the summer sun irradiates our sitting-room in the early morning. The last teaching post that she filled was as deputy head in a large, bustling school in the north. Every now and then, when I was in the area for some other purpose, she would invite me to speak at one of the morning assemblies for children at the top end of the school. Basically, she wanted them to hear something about Jesus, however obliquely the subject might be presented. That was her motivation and her quiet passion. She wanted as many people as possible to encounter the person who lived at the centre of her life.

One day, I met a man from the church where she worshipped. He told me that some of the folk in the church were 'a bit wary of Margaret'.

I couldn't help laughing. 'Wary of Margaret? Why on earth would anyone ever be wary of Margaret?'

'Ah,' said the man, 'she's a bit of a universalist, you know.'

'A bit of a what?'

'Well, you know,' he said darkly, 'she believes that everyone's going to be saved and go to heaven in the end. She says it in meetings sometimes.'

I did not prolong this discussion about my friend. I did think about what that man had said, though. I could easily imagine, knowing her as I did, that Margaret would find it difficult if not impossible to imagine any sad soul being consigned to eternal separation from God. Whether or not she was a card-carrying universalist I had no idea, but I did know that it had never prevented her from doing everything in her power over the years to introduce as many people to Jesus as possible.

Now, as I read the words of this passage, I reflect on the fact that, if Margaret is unable to accept that any will be lost, she is really only coming close to reflecting a primary facet of the heart of God. Perhaps the people in her church should be grateful to her for reminding them of something so important. Theological considerations? I dunno. Ask God.

A prayer

Father, we know that your heart breaks for those who are lost. Like Margaret, we will do all we can to bring as many as possible home to you. Thank you for those who reflect your great sorrowing love for us, and thank you for Jesus, who is the way back home to you.